Kings, Kisses, and Kickbacks

By BOBBI HARPER

Table of Contents

Chapter 1:

Kansas

I sat at the small kitchen table in the small bungalow I owned with my two sisters, Mindy and Alyssa, my laptop open and a blank document staring back at me. The aroma of freshly brewed coffee filled the air as Mindy moved around the kitchen, preparing her usual breakfast of oatmeal and fruit. Alyssa, dressed in her vibrant workout gear, was doing her morning stretches in the living room. The space was open-concept but quite small, and the decor was horribly outdated.

Mindy was humming out loud, and Alyssa had the music on just a little too loudly. I sighed and silently yelled at them to be *quiet*. It was no use. How was I supposed to get any work done when they were constantly making noise around me? Sure, I could work in my room, but it was hard to balance my laptop on my lap, and even with the extra fan underneath, it still burned my legs after too long. There was no room for a desk in the small room.

Our parents died in a house fire that destroyed our childhood home. It was determined that burning candles left unattended were the culprit of the fire. We all knew it was our mother; she loved those damned things. She'd fallen asleep while they were still burning. We had a rule in our house: no candles, *ever*. Even if I went into a store or someone else's house and smelled candles, it brought tears to my eyes. I also never bought anyone candles as a gift. Luckily, the three of us weren't home.

We did receive some money from the insurance company, but it was only enough to bury our parents and put down a moderate payment on the small bungalow we shared. The house needed a lot of work, and we were slowly chipping away at it, but money was tight for all of us.

Mindy sat down across from me, her small bowl of oatmeal topped with fresh strawberries and cinnamon— oh, how Mindy loved her cinnamon! She said it was the best ingredient to add to almost everything. And not just *any* cinnamon—it had to be *Ceylon*.

"Another article due?" Mindy asked as she sipped her coffee and then took a scoop of oatmeal.

"Yeah," I sighed, running a hand through my disheveled long black hair. "Because I know you're going to ask, this one's about urban wildlife. I just need to find the right angle."

Alyssa bounded into the kitchen, her shoulder-length black hair with pink tips swept up into a ponytail that bounced with every movement. "Good morning! Who's ready for an amazing day?" She dragged out the word 'amazing' like she was at a pep rally trying to inspire her team. She grabbed an apple, sat down, and took a big bite, her hazel eyes sparkling with enthusiasm as she crunched.

I forced a smile. "Morning, Alyssa. I'm not sure about the *amazing* part." I rolled my light gray eyes in defeat.

Alyssa shook her head. "It will only be what you make it to be," she advised.

I sighed and turned to Mindy. "You're teaching that new literature class today, right?"

Mindy nodded, her dark brown eyes thoughtful. "Yes, 'Exploring Contemporary Fiction.' I'm excited but a bit nervous. It's always a challenge to engage students with the material."

I closed my laptop, feeling the walls of the small house closing in on me. "I envy your enthusiasm. You'll do great, I'm sure. I feel like I'm in a rut. I need something new and different in my life."

Alyssa wrapped an arm around my shoulders. "You'll find it, Kansas. Your writing is amazing. Maybe you just need a change of scenery. Why don't you go to the coffee shop?"

I nodded, appreciating the support but feeling the familiar frustration bubbling beneath the surface. "Maybe. I just wish I had a place of my own. Somewhere I could truly focus."

I stood, said goodbye to them, and went to my room to put my laptop on my bed and grab my towel. A shower would surely lift my spirits and refresh me.

Later that afternoon, I sat on a park bench, my notebook open on my lap. Sometimes, unplugging myself from technology put me in a better mood. The warm Miami air swept through my hair, tousling it even more than it already was. I lifted my face to feel the heat from the sun and smiled. This was definitely what I needed.

I turned to watch a red squirrel dart up a tree and began to scribble notes about its behavior. I needed something unique for my article that would captivate my readers.

My phone buzzed with a message from my editor, Janice Tuttenham.

> Janice: Need that article by tomorrow. Countin' on you!

"Great," I muttered, rubbing my temples. I closed my eyes, trying to summon inspiration.

Suddenly, I heard a child's laughter and opened my eyes to see a little girl feeding pigeons. An idea sparked! I quickly jotted down a new angle: "The Unexpected Companions: How Urban Wildlife Brings Joy to City Life."

Excited, I began to outline my article, feeling the creative flow I'd been missing. As I wrote, I realized how much I needed moments like this—moments of solitude away from the chaos of home.

After outlining my article, I drove further into town to do my errands and spent the afternoon browsing the quaint shops of Lincoln Street. I spotted a new restaurant I'd never seen before and decided to treat myself to a nice Greek chicken souvlaki dinner.

When I returned home, the sound of laughter and chatter greeted me. Alyssa and Mindy were in the living room, watching a movie. I felt a pang of guilt for wanting to leave this lively household, but I knew it was necessary for my personal growth.

"Hey, Kansas!" Alyssa called, patting the spot next to her on the sofa. "Join us. We're watching 'The Secret Life of Pets.' Figured it might give you some ideas."

I smiled, genuinely touched. "Thanks, but I've got to finish my article. Deadline's tomorrow."

Mindy turned to me, concern in her eyes. "You okay, Kansas? You've seemed stressed lately."

I took a deep breath, deciding it was time to be honest. "I love you both, but I need my own space. I need a place where I can write without distractions, breathe, and think. I'm sure you both must feel the same way?"

Alyssa's face fell, but she nodded. "I understand. We want you to be happy and successful. Of course we both want that too."" Her eyes widened. "Wait, are you trying to tell us that you're moving out?"

I smiled, though I was sure it didn't reach my eyes. "Not right now, but I'm dreaming about it," I assured her.

"Oh, I get your pain," Mindy agreed. "I love you both, too, but it sure would be nice to have my own place."

Feeling a weight lift off my shoulders, I hugged my sisters. "Thank you for listening. I'm going to start looking for writing gigs that pay better."

I headed to my room, and instead of working on my article right away, I logged into my Amazon account and looked for a desk that I could put at the side of my bed so I could work in my room. It was a temporary solution to my problem, but it would do for now.

I normally went to bed around midnight but stayed up way too late working on my article. I wanted to get it done so it would free up some time for me to go online and find some more writing jobs to help me with my goal of saving to move out. At 3:00 a.m., I emailed my article to Janice and headed to bed for a restless sleep.

***

I gave up trying to sleep around 7 a.m., too wired to fall back asleep, and just laid there thinking about how I needed to bring in more money so I could get my own place. I rarely slept through the night, especially lately. I always had too much on my mind and couldn't seem to shut it off. I tried various sleeping techniques and found that sometimes visualization worked for me. It didn't this time, which was unfortunate, but I wasn't willing to try any type of drugs.

Since I was in the kitchen getting a glass of water, I put Mindy's pot of coffee on for her and took my water outside on the back deck. The three of us had spent a weekend planting flowers and a lilac tree, which was beautiful. I especially loved the climbing roses that covered the fences. It dawned on me then that I could bring my laptop outside to work. Why hadn't I ever thought of that before? I laughed at myself.

I went back inside to retrieve my laptop, and as if on cue, Mindy entered, her glasses perched on her nose and a stack of papers in her hands. "Morning, Kansas. I've got lots of essays to grade today. What are you doing up already?"

"Morning, Mindy. I'm just trying to get a head start on the day," I replied, a hint of weariness in my voice.

Mindy poured herself some coffee and sat at the table observing me. "You look tired. Late night writing?"

I nodded. "Yeah, I was working on my urban wildlife article. Got it done and sent it to my boss, Janice."

"She really drives you hard, doesn't she?" Mindy asked.

"It's good. I do better with deadlines."

Before Mindy could respond, Alyssa bounded into the kitchen, her energy infectious even at this early hour. "Good morning, sisters!" she chirped, grabbing her daily apple. "I'm ready for another day of making people sweat and smile."

I smiled at Alyssa's enthusiasm, though a pang of envy tugged at my heart. She seemed to thrive in her role as a personal trainer.

"I'd better get going," Mindy said as she stood and gathered her papers. "My first class starts in an hour."

She left with Alyssa trailing behind her to go teach an aerobics class at the gym.

On my way to the magazine, which was about a 30-minute drive, my hands gripped the steering wheel as I made my way through the rush-hour traffic. The purple Jeep Wrangler had been my constant companion for years, but today, an unfamiliar clanking sound cut through the engine's steady drone. My heart sank. The sound grew louder when I accelerated. I could feel the stress tightening in my chest, my mind racing with thoughts of repair bills and the possibility of being stranded on the side of the road.

Thankfully, I made it to work, and the second I got to my office, I called my mechanic. He offered to come and pick it up, so I didn't have to drive to his shop and back to work. I was lucky that Frank did special favors for me like that, and I knew I could trust him not to rip me off.

I sat at my desk, typing in some ideas for my next article, when Willow Tozzier, my close friend and colleague, breezed into the room. As usual, she had a travel bag slung over her shoulder. Her long, thick, straight blond hair looked like a sheet of silky shredded wheat as it hung to her waist. She sat on the chair across from me and rested her legs on the edge of my desk.

"Make yourself at home," I said sarcastically with a shake of my head.

"What? It's comfortable," Willow said with a grin. She fixed her big gray-blue eyes on me. "You look like you've got the weight of the world on your shoulders. Everything okay?"

I forced a smile. "Just car troubles. There's a strange sound, so Frank's going to look at it for me. I'm stressing over how much the bill is going to be. I'm trying so hard to save to buy my own place," I said with a heavy sigh. "I feel like it's never going to happen."

"You know what you need? A vacation. Seriously, come with me on one of my assignments. You've been cooped up here for too long. It would be good for you to get out and see some different parts of the world."

My mind wandered to the idea of an exotic getaway, but reality quickly pulled me back. "That sounds amazing, but I can't afford it right now."

Willow's expression softened, but then she snapped her fingers, her eyes sparkling with excitement. "Wait, I've got it! Why don't you pitch to Zuri that you expand your column? You're already writing about animals—why not take it global? You could do pieces on animals in different countries, which would involve some travel. They'd cover your costs, and you'd get to explore new places. Win-win!"

I blinked, considering the idea. It was bold and something I hadn't thought of before. "That's actually a great idea. I mean, it's a bit of a long shot, but it could work. I've certainly proved myself worthy, and it would get me out of this rut. Do you think Zuri would agree to it?"

"Of course, he would! It would mean more copies sold. And it will increase your salary by a lot." Willow winked.

"Oh, really? Now, that would be worth it." I felt hopeful. "I'll put together a proposal."

"Anytime," Willow said warmly. "And hey, if it works out, we might even end up on the same trip. Just imagine all the stories we could come back with!"

Willow got up and left as fast as she had arrived, and I was left with several thoughts swirling around my brain.

Several hours later, I sat across from Zuri Diamini, my boss, in his spacious office. He had called me in for a meeting. Zuri leaned forward, his fingers steepled as he met my gaze. "I've got quite an opportunity for you. One that could change your life—and your career."

I raised an eyebrow, my curiosity piqued. "What is it?"

"A good friend of mine, Dawson Lancaster—I'm sure you've heard of him—owns a successful hotel chain. He's decided it's time to tell his story, to have a biography written about his journey to success. He asked me if I knew of anyone who could take on the project, and immediately I thought of you. I know you usually focus on animals, but this would be a great opportunity for you to expand your writing abilities."

I blinked, taken aback. "You want me to write his biography?" I was quite shocked.

Zuri leaned back and nodded. He tilted his head and ran his long fingers along his black beard, his black eyes gazing into mine with excitement. He had gotten his Afro cut back so that it was only about an inch long now, with zigzag patterns running along the sides. His expensive gray silk suit fit him perfectly, accentuating his long, lean body. I loved the accent of the burgundy tie.

He looked like he just finished a photoshoot with Versace.

"Yes, I think you're a perfect candidate for it. You have a way with words, Kansas, and you know how to dig deep to find the heart of a story. This could be huge for you and the magazine. I trust you to make it a great article."

I felt my pulse quicken. This was big. Huge! "This sounds incredible, Zuri, but what's the catch?"

Zuri's expression turned more serious. "There is one thing—Dawson insists that whoever writes his story lives with him for the duration of the project. I know it sounds strange, but he wants full access, someone who can immerse themselves into his world by truly understanding his life. He wants to capture the real essence of him in the article. It's non-negotiable."

I frowned, my mind racing uncontrollably. Move in with Dawson Lancaster? The man was everything I couldn't stand—lavishly wealthy, living in a massive mansion, and spending money on things that seemed so insignificant to me. I'd seen the media portrayals, and none of it sat well with me. "Living with him?" I echoed as I tried to keep the disbelief out of my voice.

"Yes," Zuri confirmed. "I know it's a lot to ask, but this is a once-in-a-lifetime opportunity. If you pull this off, not only will it be a major feather in your cap, but there's also a substantial payout. One hundred thousand dollars."

My breath caught. *One hundred thousand dollars?* That kind of money could change everything for me and my sisters. We could sell the house, pool all the money together, and finally buy our own places. I could finally breathe!

Zuri saw the wheels turning and pressed on. "I know Dawson's not your favorite person, and I get why you might have reservations about this. But this is a chance to kick start your career in a lucrative way. And let's be honest, the money alone could really help you out, right?"

I looked at my hands in my lap, the weight of this decision settling over me. I needed the money—badly. And as much as I despised everything Dawson Lancaster seemed to stand for, I couldn't deny that this was an opportunity I couldn't afford to pass up.

I looked up, meeting Zuri's eyes with a firm nod. "I'll do it. I'll write his biography." I almost choked on the words.

Zuri's smile widened, relief evident in his eyes. "I knew you would. This is going to be big, Kansas. For you, for the magazine—hell, for everyone who reads it. You're the best person for this job, and I have no doubt you'll make it a great success."

I forced a smile, trying to push aside my apprehensions. "Thanks, Zuri. I'll give it everything I've got."

As I left Zuri's office, the reality of what I'd just agreed to washed over me in waves of panic. I was about to move in with a man who embodied everything I couldn't stand, all for the sake of a job I desperately needed. It wasn't going to be easy, but with one hundred thousand dollars on the line, I knew I had no other choice.

This was my chance to change my life—and my sister's lives—and I was determined to make the most of it, no matter how awful it got.

Frank called and brought my car back, and I was relieved when he told me it was just the bushings that needed to be replaced, which only cost me $300. I thanked him and drove over to the florist shop where my best friend, Shellene Cosgrove, worked as the manager.

I caught sight of Shellene's bright red hair over in the flower freezer and opened the door. "Playing with flowers again, are you?" I teased.

Shellene's porcelain face beamed back at me. "Hey, girl. So, what brings you to my floral paradise? Need to buy a special arrangement?"

"No, I'm here for you. I thought we could grab some coffee and catch up. I feel like I haven't seen you in forever!"

"It's been crazy. Actually, I've got something to tell you," Shellene informed me as she walked around the counter to take her apron off.

"This sounds serious. What's going on?"

"Let's go down the street and sit at the cafe and talk. I can take half an hour." Her dark blue eyes flashed with excitement.

"Deal. Let's go!"

We sat down five minutes later and continued our conversation.

"My boss is putting the shop up for sale," Shellene announced.

"No way! That place has been here a long time. I wonder what's going to happen to it."

"I've been thinking," Shellene said shyly. "I might try to buy it."

I stared at my friend as I processed the news. "Are you serious? That's amazing! Running a business is a whole different ballgame to what you're used to."

Shellene shrugged. "I know, and it's terrifying but also exciting. I've been saving up and running this place for eight years now. I think I can make it work. It feels like the right time, you know? I love it here and all my longtime clients."

"That's huge. I'm so proud of you. You'll make it work. I know you will," I encouraged her.

Shellene blushed. "Enough about me. What's going on with you?"

"I accepted a job! A big one. I'm going to write a book."

Shellene's eyes widened in surprise. "A book? About what?"

"About who," I corrected her. "It's for this billionaire guy. He wants me to write a book about his life and his success story. It's totally out of my comfort zone, but it's a huge opportunity. Plus, it pays really well. Maybe even enough to get my own place."

"Kansas, that's incredible! You've always wanted a project more substantial than your column. I know you love writing about animals, but this could be life-changing."

"I'm a little nervous. This guy is kind of intimidating and not my kind of person."

"Who is it?"

"Dawson Lancaster."

"Dawson Lancaster?" Shellene echoed, her eyes doubling in size. She blew out a low whistle and raised her eyebrows. "Are you sure you'll be able to handle being around him?"

"Well, that's where the bad news comes in. I have to move in with him for the duration of the project."

"What? You've got to be kidding! That will crush you. You've always disliked people like him. It's nauseating how privileged his kind of people are."

I shrugged. "I will just deal with it, I guess. I need the money, or I probably wouldn't do it."

"Wow. It sounds like we're both going to be up for a challenge. We can do it!" Shellene said encouragingly.

"We sure can," I agreed.

But when I got home later, my mind was spinning. I lay awake thinking about it and wondered if I was making a big mistake. I had no idea how I was going to spend time living with a man I already despised. I reminded myself that this was just a job and I had worked with other people I didn't like. This couldn't be that much different, could it?

Chapter 2:

Dawson

Dinner at my parents' house is always a blend of grandeur and tradition. The elaborate spread of dishes laid out on the dining room table—my mom insisted on formal dinners every Sunday evening—made me wonder just how many different dishes she'd prepared. Food was her thing.

My father, Fred, sat at the head of the table, content and proud as always, his salt and pepper hair combed back, and he wore the same confident smile I remembered from my childhood. He was the calm in the storm, the man who built the foundation I took to new heights. To his right was my younger brother, Preston, freshly pressed in his police uniform, ever the hero, with that steady resolve that made him the rock in any crisis. And then there was my other younger brother, Hutton, across from me, relaxed as usual, leaning back in his chair with an easy grin, talking about the latest holistic techniques he was implementing in his massage therapy business.

And, of course, there was my mom, Lorraine, at the other end, eyes sharp as a hawk as she surveyed her brood. She had that aura of authority, and tonight, it was directed squarely at me.

"Dawson, darling," she said, slicing through the tension with a sweet tone that I knew all too well. "Have you given any thought to settling down? You know, finding a nice girl to share your life with? I hear Lara Robertson is still available. She was so perfect."

I knew this was coming. She'd been hinting at it for months, dropping not-so-subtle comments about family, legacy, and my supposed need for a partner, especially Lara, my ex-girlfriend. I set down my fork, carefully placing it next to my plate, and met her gaze.

"Mother," I said, keeping my voice even, "Lara and I will never marry, so you can forget about that immediately. Besides, I'm focused on the business right now. Lancaster Luxury Estates is growing faster than ever, and that requires all my attention."

Her smile faltered just slightly, and she glanced at Preston, who was already digging into his meal like this conversation wasn't happening.

"Preston has a girlfriend," she said, her tone light but with an edge I couldn't ignore. "And Hutton, too. Both your brothers have found time for relationships despite their busy schedules. Don't you think it's time you did the same?"

I resisted the urge to sigh. "I'm not Preston or Hutton, Mother. I'm Dawson. My priorities are different. I have responsibilities that go beyond—"

"Beyond what, dear?" she interrupted, her voice sharp now. "Beyond a family? Beyond your future happiness? You can't tell me you're planning to be alone forever."

"It's not about being alone," I countered, feeling the familiar frustration rise. "It's about making sure the business is secure and that everything Dad worked for is not just maintained but expanded. I'm not ready to settle down because I'm focusing on making sure our legacy continues to grow."

There was an awkward silence, thick with tension, before Hutton jumped in, always the peacemaker.

"Mom, Dawson's doing what he loves. You know how much he's put into Lancaster Luxury Estates. It's not like he's avoiding a relationship—he's just waiting for the right time. Right, Dawson?"

I nodded, grateful for his attempt to defuse the situation. "Exactly. The right time."

But Lorraine wasn't satisfied. She never was when she set her mind on something.

"Time has a way of slipping past us, Dawson," she sighed quietly, almost to herself. "I just don't want you to wake up one day and realize you've missed something important."

Preston finally looked up, wiping his mouth with a napkin. "Mom, Dawson knows what he's doing. If there's one thing we all learned from Dad, it's that you must follow your own path and make your own decisions. He's doing that, just like Hutton and I are."

"But neither of you wants anything to do with the hotel business," she retorted, her voice laced with frustration. "Dawson's carrying this burden alone, and it worries me.

A good woman by his side could help ground him. A good woman like Lara Robertson."

"Mother," I said, more firmly now, "I appreciate your concern, but I'm not interested in comparisons or *Lara Robertson*. Preston and Hutton have their lives, and I have mine. The business is my focus, and I'll find someone when the time is right. But it will be on my terms."

Fred finally chimed in, his voice calm and measured. "Lorraine, let the boy be. He's made more of Lancaster Luxury Estates than any of us could have imagined. He'll know when the time is right."

Lorraine's lips pressed into a thin line, but she nodded, relenting for now. "I'm just looking out for my son."

"No need, Mom. I can handle my own relationships just fine." I picked up my fork again, signaling the end of the conversation. The tension lingered, but the subject was dropped.

As dinner continued, with Preston talking about a recent homicide case and Hutton detailing a new massage technique he'd perfected, I couldn't help but feel the weight of my mother's words. But I pushed it aside. There was no room for distractions. Not now, when I was so close to taking Lancaster Luxury Estates to the next level.

Family, legacy, love—they're all important. But I felt business came first.

After dinner, I followed my father onto the back patio, the night air warm and heavy. Fred sipped his scotch, his eyes on the horizon. I knew what was coming before he even spoke.

"Dawson," he began, his voice steady but probing, "I've been thinking about the expansion plans you mentioned. Are you sure this is the right move? International markets are unpredictable, and you're taking on a lot of risk."

I clenched my jaw, keeping my tone measured. "Dad, I've run the numbers. The demand is there, and it's a strategic move. We can't stay stagnant."

Fred nodded slowly, but I could see the doubt in his eyes. "You know, sometimes sticking to what you know is better than chasing the next big thing. It's how I built this business—careful steps, not leaps."

I bit back my frustration. "And I've taken those careful steps, but times have changed. We need to innovate to stay ahead."

He sighed, swirling his drink. "I just don't want you to lose everything we've built by pushing too hard, too fast."

I could feel my anger rising, the unspoken jealousy. "I'm not losing anything, Dad. I'm building on what you started, taking it further. But I have to do it my way."

After the stressful conversation with Dad, I found myself in the study with Preston and Hutton, nursing a glass of bourbon. The room was dimly lit, the warm glow from the fireplace casting flickering shadows on the walls. Preston was leaning against the mantle, arms crossed, while Hutton was slouched in one of the leather chairs, looking thoughtful.

"I just don't get it," I said, breaking the silence. "No matter what I do, it feels like Dad is never satisfied. It's like he's stuck in the past, unwilling to see that times have changed."

Preston, always the straightforward one, nodded. "Look, Dawson, you've taken Lancaster Luxury Estates to levels none of us could have imagined. The numbers speak for themselves. You're right to trust your instincts. If you keep trying to please Dad, you'll hold yourself back."

Hutton sighed, sitting up a little. "I get what you're saying, Preston, but I think there's more to it. Dad ran the business successfully for a long time. He knows a thing or two, and maybe his caution isn't such a bad thing. Sometimes, it's about keeping the peace and listening to his words. There might be some good advice, even if it's wrapped up in his old-school mentality."

Preston shook his head, a smirk playing on his lips. "You're just saying that because you hate conflict, Hutton. But Dawson's right. Today's business world isn't what it was when Dad was running things. We have to adapt, or we'll get left behind."

Hutton shrugged, conceding a little. "Maybe, but that doesn't mean you must completely dismiss what Dad says."

I stared into my glass, then looked at Hutton. "I know you're both right, in a way. But it's frustrating. I respect our father, but can't keep running everything by him. I must do this my way, even if it means clashing with him."

Preston clapped me on the shoulder. "Then do it, Dawson. You've got this."

Hutton nodded, more subdued. "Just don't burn any bridges along the way. You'll find the balance."

I nodded, appreciating their support, even if they disagreed. It was good to have brothers who understood, even if they had different ways of seeing things.

On the drive home, my mind raced with everything that had been discussed at my parents' house. I sighed. Every time I left their place, I always felt somewhat deflated. I needed something to take my mind off them, so I called my best friend, Ritter Martindale, and asked him to come over to play some pool. He told me he would be right over.

Ritter arrived at my place just as the sun was beginning to set. He strolled in all swagger and grinning like he owned the place, picking up a cue stick in one hand and a beer in the other.

"Ready to get your ass kicked?" he quipped, his eyes twinkling with mischief.

I smirked, grabbing one of the beers as I led him to the game room. "You wish, Martindale. I've been practicing."

Ritter chuckled as we set up the table, his laughter infectious as always. "You know, Dawson, if you put as much effort into finding a girlfriend as you do perfecting your break shot, your mom might finally get off your back."

I rolled my eyes, lining up my shot. "You sound just like her. It's like everyone thinks I need a woman to distract me from work."

Ritter leaned against the table, watching me closely. "Maybe because it's true. You're wound tighter than a drum. And don't tell me this is about Lara again. That's ancient history, man."

I paused, the mention of Lara bringing back a flood of memories I'd rather forget. "It's not that simple, Ritter. She tried to take me for everything I had. Two years of my life wasted on someone who only cared about my bank account. Then she sued me when I finally saw through her, and the whole damn thing became a media circus. I certainly won't make that mistake again!"

Ritter sighed, his usual playful demeanor softening. "Yeah, I remember. But that was *one* woman, Dawson. You can't let her ruin it for everyone else. Not all of them are out to get you."

I took a swig of my beer, feeling the bitterness rising. "It's not just about Lara. It's the whole damn package. The media loves to paint me as the villain, and I'm sick of it."

Ritter raised an eyebrow. "Is that why you're considering hiring someone to write your story? Put it all out there, no filters?"

"Exactly," I said, sinking the eight ball with a satisfying crack. "I talked to my buddy, Zuri, about it. I'm done with the media twisting everything. If my story's out there, on my terms, maybe they'll finally get it right."

Ritter nodded, considering this. "But are you sure you want to open that can of worms? You've been pretty private about your life. Putting it all out there could stir up a lot of old crap."

"I know," I admitted, setting my cue stick down. "But I'm tired of hiding. The truth is better than their lies, even if it means facing the past."

Ritter grinned, clapping me on the back. "Well, if anyone can spin a tale worth telling, it's you. Just make sure you add a chapter about getting out of your own way and letting a good woman in."

I snorted, shaking my head as we headed outside to the pool. "Not happening, Ritter. Not after Lara. I don't trust the female race."

Ritter just laughed, diving into the pool with a splash. "We'll see, Lancaster. We'll see."

After Ritter left a few hours later, I sat at my desk, eying the list of names I'd jotted down earlier. Helena Holt, Jordan Phillips, and Kansas Stonehouse. Each one had their merits, but my gut told me where I was leaning. Helena was renowned for writing biographies of top-tier celebrities, but something about her felt too polished. Next was Jordan. He was solid—he'd just finished a biography for one of my friends, but honestly, I didn't want a man writing my story. Then there was Kansas—

an interesting name. Her pet column always cracked me up. Her energy and wit jumped off the page. I could already tell she'd be a handful, but maybe that was precisely what I needed. She seemed like quite a firecracker. If anyone could capture my journey in a fresh way, it would be her.

Chapter 3:

Kansas

I stood in front of the mirror, smoothing the wrinkles out of my blouse for what felt like the hundredth time. My stomach churned with nerves and resentment. The idea of working for Dawson Lancaster, the man who owned half of Miami's skyline, made my blood boil. I had spent my entire life scraping by, and now I was supposed to sit across from a man who had everything handed to him on a silver platter.

"Kansas, stop fidgeting," Mindy said, her voice calm and steady as always. She was perched on the edge of my bed, her legs crossed neatly. "You're going to do great. Just focus on the job, not the person."

"That's easy for you to say," I muttered, adjusting my collar. "You don't have to deal with *him*."

Alyssa, who had been sitting on the floor painting her toenails, looked up with wide, innocent eyes. "What if he's nice? Maybe he's not as bad as you think. Plus, he's handsome and sexy."

I snorted, unable to help myself. "Nice? A billionaire who probably thinks he can buy anything he wants, including people? No thanks, and I really don't care what he looks like!"

Alyssa's brows furrowed in concern. "But you can't let your personal feelings get in the way, Kansas. This is a big opportunity."

"I know," I sighed, running a hand through my hair. "I just don't want to mess this up. But I can't stop wondering who else he's interviewing. What if I'm just one of many? What if I'm not good enough?"

Mindy stood up, her expression softening as she touched my shoulder reassuringly. "You are good enough. And don't worry about the others. Just be yourself. You're a creator, Kansas. Use that to your advantage."

I nodded, trying to absorb her confidence. "You're right. I just have to get through this. And pray I don't punch him in the face."

Alyssa giggled, and even Mindy cracked a smile. But as I gathered my things and headed out the door, the weight of the interview settled back onto my shoulders. I just hoped to keep my true feelings buried deep enough to get through it without ruining everything.

***

The moment I stepped through the wrought iron gates of Dawson Lancaster's estate, I felt a sinking sensation in the pit of my stomach. The mansion loomed ahead, a sprawling testament to wealth and excess, with pristine lawns that seemed to stretch on forever. I hesitated, wondering if I'd made a mistake accepting this interview. I had grown up scrimping and saving, and now here I was, about to sit down with a man who probably spent more on landscaping in a month than I'd earned in a year.

As I approached the front entrance, the doors swung open almost magically. I half expected the whole house to be automated, but instead, I was greeted by a butler of all things. He was dressed in a crisp black suit, looking every bit the part of someone who served the elite.

"Miss Stonehouse?" His voice was smooth, polished, and utterly unruffled as if I were just another guest at the mansion. He saluted me, and I couldn't help but notice his pleasant smile. He reminded me of Bryan Cranston—only a few inches taller.

I smiled warmly, trying not to gape at the luxury around me. The foyer was massive, with marble floors that gleamed under the crystal chandeliers. I had never seen anything so lavish in my life. It made me feel small and insignificant.

"If you'll follow me, please," the butler said, leading me through the maze of hallways. As we walked, I couldn't help but notice the sheer size of the place. Room after room, each more extravagant than the last. It was overwhelming, and I felt a twinge of envy. What would it be like to live in a place like this? To never worry about money or where your next meal was coming from?

We passed the kitchen, where a woman in a crisp white apron bustled about. She glanced up as we entered and smiled warmly. "Would you like anything to eat, Miss?" she asked, her tone genuinely hospitable. Her bright blue eyes looked so kind, and when she smiled, it made me want to stay and talk to her.

"Tea would be nice, thank you," I said.

The woman nodded and busied herself with the task as the butler led me to a sitting room that was larger than my house's entire first floor. As I waited, more servants came and went, each carrying out some small task as if Dawson was too important to lift a finger for himself. The audacity of it all made my blood boil. Who needed this many people just to keep a house running? Or rather, an oversized mansion.

When Dawson finally appeared, my heart did an involuntary flip. I hated myself for it, but there was something about the way he carried himself, with that smug confidence, that sent a shiver down my spine. He was tall, with chiseled features, and dressed in a suit that probably cost more than my car. His eyes were so dark they were almost black, but they also seemed kind, and when he looked at me, it was as if he could see right through me. He was the cliché of tall, dark, handsome, and then some.

"Miss Stonehouse," he said, his voice rich and deep, with just a hint of amusement.

I forced a smile, trying to keep my composure. "Thank you for the opportunity, Mr. Lancaster."

He gestured for me to sit, and I sat across from him, feeling strangely vulnerable under his intense gaze. As we started talking, I couldn't help but notice he had an air of entitlement that made me want to punch him. Yet, there was also something devilish and sly in his smile that I found annoyingly attractive. I chastised myself for even thinking it, but it was there.

"So, Miss Stonehouse," he began, leaning forward slightly, his eyes locked on mine. "Why do you want to write my biography?"

I opened my mouth to respond, but the words caught in my throat. He was insufferable, yet I couldn't deny the attraction that buzzed between us like a live wire. I pushed it down, reminding myself why I was there and who he was. This man represented everything I despised about the ultra-rich, and no amount of devilish charm could change that. But as he continued to stare into my eyes, I couldn't help but shiver. This was going to be much more complicated than I'd thought.

"You're only doing this for the money, aren't you?" Dawson leaned back in his chair, his eyes narrowing as he studied me. His voice dripped with condescension, and it set my teeth on edge.

I crossed my arms, meeting his gaze without flinching. "Excuse me?"

"You heard me," he said, a smirk playing at the corner of his mouth. "You don't believe I have a great story to tell. You're just here for the paycheck."

I scoffed, feeling the heat rise in my cheeks. "Please. I'd never work with you for all the money in the world." I stood up. "This was a big mistake. Thank you for your time."

He arched an eyebrow, clearly amused by my response. "Is that so? Sit down," he ordered.

I clenched my fists, forcing myself to stay calm. "You think you're so special, don't you? That everyone around you is just a pawn in your little game. Well, I'm not interested in playing."

Dawson's smirk faded, replaced by a harder, more calculating look. "Be careful, Kansas. You might find that walking away from this job is the biggest mistake of your life."

"Maybe," I shot back, my voice trembling slightly despite my best efforts. "But I'd rather make that mistake than sell my soul to someone like you."

Without giving him a chance to respond, I turned and walked out of the room, my heart pounding in my chest. As soon as I was outside, the reality of what I'd done hit me like a freight train. What had I just done?

I needed that job—desperately—and now I'd thrown it away. The humiliation and panic began to set in as I hurried to my car, my mind racing. I couldn't believe I'd let my pride get the better of me. What was I going to do now? How did that even happen?

***

I sat across from Willow at our favorite little bistro, stirring my drink absentmindedly. The words I'd exchanged with Dawson earlier replayed in my head like a broken record. Willow's intense gray-blue eyes watched me, waiting for me to spill everything. I finally sighed and blurted it all out—the fight, the anger, the stupid pride that had me walking away from what could've been the biggest opportunity of my career.

When I finished, Willow leaned back in her chair, shaking her head. "Kansas, you're crazy," she said, her voice laced with disbelief. "You're seriously going to turn down that kind of money? And possible fame? For what, your pride?"

"It's not just about pride," I protested, but even as the words left my mouth, I knew how hollow they sounded. "He's insufferable, Willow. I can't stand the guy."

"So what?" Willow said, her tone blunt. "Sometimes you just have to suck it up and do it anyway. Think of your sisters. You've been talking about how you all need your own place. This job could make that happen."

I frowned, the reality of her words hitting me hard. "I know, but—"

"No buts," Willow interrupted, her eyes narrowing in determination. "You need that money. You need it to pay bills, to give you and your sisters some breathing room. You're not just doing this for yourself, Kansas. This is bigger than that."

I stared at her, the entire weight of what I'd done crashing down on me. She was right. I'd let my personal feelings cloud my judgment, and in doing so, I'd potentially sabotaged not just my future but my sisters' as well.

"Look," Willow continued, her tone softening, "I get it. Dawson's a jerk. But that doesn't mean you can't make something good out of this. Sometimes, the hardest thing is the right thing to do."

I nodded slowly, the panic I'd felt earlier giving way to a new resolve. "You're right," I admitted. "I can't let this opportunity slip away. I'll call him tomorrow and apologize. I'll try to fix this."

Willow smiled, a knowing look in her eyes. "That's the Kansas I know. You've got this."

Her words settled in my heart, and I knew she was right. I had to do this, not just for myself but for the people who depended on me. No matter how much I despised Dawson, I couldn't let this chance go to waste.

***

When I walked through the door a few hours later, I immediately heard Mindy's exasperated voice coming from the living room. "Alyssa, you can't just leave your stuff everywhere! We're running out of space!"

Alyssa's soft reply followed, "I'm sorry, I just don't have anywhere else to put it."

I sighed, leaning against the wall as their voices drifted through the house. This constant tension was wearing on all of us.

I knew then that I didn't have a choice. I had to work with Dawson, no matter how much I couldn't stand him. I had to do it for them. Now, I just had to get Dawson to forgive me for turning him down so rudely!

Chapter 4:

Dawson

The day was sweltering, typical Miami summer. I sat behind my mahogany desk, the air conditioning futilely battling the heat, preparing to meet the second candidate for the position.

She walked in with a forced smile and a firm handshake. "Good morning, Mr. Dawson. I'm Alyssa Hughes." She was a woman in her mid-forties, dressed conservatively yet dated, and her dirty blond hair was perfectly styled. Very nicely put together, but I found her uninteresting.

I gestured to the chair across from me. "Please, have a seat."

As she settled in, I couldn't shake the sense of déjà vu— another cookie-cutter interview. Alyssa was the textbook definition of safe. Her responses were well-rehearsed, and her demeanor was immaculate but dull. I couldn't imagine her making waves or adding a spark to my success story with Lancaster Luxury Estates.

"So, Alyssa," I began, "tell me about a time you overcame a significant challenge in your career." Even as I asked her the question, I knew I wasn't interested in her answer.

She smiled a bit too widely and leaned forward. "Well, there was this one project where—"

I tuned her out as she recounted her story in monotonous detail. Her passion was absent, replaced by a predictable script of achievements. My mind wandered to Kansas, who I'd interviewed earlier. Her fire and edge were impossible to forget. Her scathing critique of the ultra-rich, especially me, was almost refreshing in its audacity.

I forced myself to pay attention as Alyssa finished her tale. "Thank you for sharing," I said, though my tone lacked enthusiasm. "We'll be in touch."

She left with a polite nod, and I exhaled, relieved. I knew my choice already. The thrill of Kansas's irreverence was more appealing than the comfort of Alyssa's predictability. The idea of having someone like Kansas shake things up seemed precisely what I needed to break the monotony of my *ultra-rich* existence.

***

I looked out the window as I waited for Kansas to arrive. I wanted to see what vehicle she drove up in. I smiled when I saw her drive up in the purple Jeep Wrangler. *Of course.* It truly suited her personality. Her earlier defiance had intrigued me more than I cared to admit.

When she finally walked through the door, I was struck by the contrast she presented. Her presence was understated but undeniably captivating. She wore a simple, flowing white dress that accentuated her grace in a way that was both subtle and arresting.

"Mr. Dawson," she greeted, her tone calm but polite, and a smile did not accompany the greeting. She took a seat opposite my desk, her posture relaxed but assertive.

"Please, call me Dawson," I said, motioning for her to sit. "I wanted to have another discussion with you. After considering our last conversation, I've decided I'd like to offer you the position."

Kansas held my gaze, but her eyes narrowed slightly, and she looked stunned. She obviously hadn't expected that I would offer her the position. "I appreciate the offer, but I'm afraid I'm not interested."

I leaned back, trying to hide my surprise. "I see. Why did you come here then, if you're not interested? You could have just emailed me. What if I upped the offer to two hundred thousand dollars? It's quite a generous sum."

Her expression remained unchanged, though I could see a flicker of curiosity in her eyes. "That's a lot of money, but it doesn't change my feelings about the job."

I was intrigued by her stoicism. Most people would have jumped at the chance for such an offer, but Kansas remained unmoved. "Just what are your feelings, and what would it take for you to reconsider?" I asked, genuinely curious.

She hesitated, her eyes scanning the room before meeting mine again. "I'm not sure money is the issue here. I need to believe in what I'm doing."

Her honesty was both refreshing and frustrating. I was accustomed to people who either fawned over my wealth or tried to manipulate me. Kansas, however, operated on her own terms, and it intrigued me.

"I can respect that," I said, leaning forward, my tone softening. "But I'd like to understand what makes you tick. I don't come across people like you often. If there's something you need, I'm willing to listen."

She looked at me momentarily, studying my face as if searching for sincerity. "And why should I believe you?"

"Because," I said, meeting her gaze steadily, "I'm not used to people who don't play games. I value authenticity. I want someone who can challenge me, not just be a minion."

There was a brief silence. Kansas' composure wavered slightly, and I caught a glimpse of vulnerability beneath her strong exterior. It was a rare sight, and it made me even more determined to bring her on board.

"I need to be honest," she began, her voice steady. "I'm not sure I could live with you. It's not just about the job—the living arrangement concerns me."

I studied her, my curiosity piqued. "I understand your reservations, Kansas, but that part is non-negotiable. My schedule isn't typical. I have strange hours and need someone to be there when inspiration strikes. Essentially, when I'm available to work, I will need you there at exactly the moment it strikes me. I don't have time to waste on waiting for you to arrive or answer my message."

Her brow furrowed, clearly wrestling with the idea. "So, you're saying you need me to be on-call around the clock?"

"Yes," I replied, leaning forward. "I'll need your presence and input extensively. We'll be collaborating closely, often at unconventional times."

She sighed, the weight of the situation settling on her shoulders. "That sounds like a lot to ask."

"I agree, it is. But it's essential for the project. I need someone who can match my drive and dedication. I believe my offer of two hundred thousand is more than fair for any inconvenience you might face while working with me."

She looked down, seemingly lost in thought. Her determination was visible, and it was clear she was struggling with the implications. I admired her resolve, a rare quality that drew me to her even more.

"Look," I said, softening my tone. "I know this isn't what you planned. But if you can look past the inconvenience, I believe this could be an opportunity for us to create something exceptional."

Her beautiful light gray eyes met mine again, a spark of consideration flickering. "I'll think about it." This time, she sounded more like she meant it.

I nodded, feeling relieved but still full of anticipation. I was drawn to her honesty, a rare quality these days, but she also promised to bring a new dynamic to my life— and my project.

Kansas sat still, contemplating my offer. Her posture was relaxed, but her mind was clearly racing. The grand room seemed to close in around us, and I savored the tension in the air.

"You say you need time to think," I began, keeping my tone casual but firm. "However, I must inform you that if you walk out of here without giving me an answer, it will show me that your desire to rise to this challenge is misplaced, which means I'll have no choice but to offer the job to the second candidate I interviewed." I shuddered at the thought but held her gaze firm.

Her eyes widened slightly, surprise and irritation crossing her features. "So, you're trying to pressure me into making this decision right now?"

I leaned back, feigning nonchalance. "Consider it a motivational tool. I need to know if you're fully committed. I'm not prepared to wait while you go think about it."

Her gaze shifted to the floor as she mulled over my words. I watched her, fascinated by the inner battle behind her calm exterior. Her reluctance to cave into my tactics only made her more intriguing. While it would be a disappointment, the idea of her walking away wouldn't change my mind. However, I became more invested in her response with every passing second.

"I don't appreciate being cornered," she said tersely, looking up with a steely resolve. "But I do appreciate *your* honesty."

Her words were clipped, but I could see the wheels turning in her mind. I liked that she wasn't easily swayed and made me work for it. There was something about her that demanded my attention and respect.

"I understand your frustration," I said, trying to soften my stance because I really did want her to take the job. "But this is a significant project, and I need someone who can handle both the pressure and its unpredictable nature. I believe you're that person."

She took a deep breath, her eyes meeting mine with defiance and contemplation. "You're asking for a lot, Dawson."

"I am," I admitted, nodding. "But you're the only one who's shown the kind of passion and creativity I'm looking for. Even if you choose to walk away, I'd still want to work with you."

The room was silent, the weight of my words hanging in the air. I could see the internal struggle in her eyes, and it was challenging and exhilarating to witness. If she agreed, I vowed to discover what she despised about me.

"If I agree," she said slowly, "what guarantees do I have that this will remain professional?"

I laughed. "*That's* what you're worried about?" I asked with a smirk. "Believe me, I have *zero* intention of crossing any boundaries with you," I replied honestly. And I didn't. I had no time in my life for that kind of thing. "I promise it will be a dynamic, challenging experience. I've seen enough to know that you have the potential to bring something extraordinary to this project."

Kansas's expression remained guarded. "Alright," she said finally, her voice steady. "I'll take the job. But only if we can establish clear boundaries and expectations."

"Deal," I said, a genuine smile forming. "Welcome aboard, Kansas."

As she stood to leave, I couldn't help but feel a surge of anticipation. Kansas had intrigued me from the start, and now that she was officially going to be moving in and writing my book, I knew I needed to delve deeper into what made her tick. The challenge of understanding her—of unraveling the enigma she presented—was precisely what I needed to spice up my life.

After Kansas left, I felt a rare surge of excitement. There was something invigorating about how she challenged me, her fiery spirit promising to shake things up in ways I hadn't anticipated.

I decided to take advantage of the early evening warmth, heading out to unwind with my Dobermans and a swim. The moment I stepped onto the expansive patio, my two Dobermans bounded toward me, their tails wagging vigorously. I ruffled their ears and tossed a few tennis balls for them to chase.

As I watched them race around, I couldn't help but think about Kansas. I wondered if she liked dogs. The thought made me grin. There was something amusing about the idea of this fiery, no-nonsense woman interacting with my well-trained but still boisterous companions. Perhaps she'd appreciate their loyalty and energy, or maybe she'd cringe and make a face. Either way, it added a layer of curiosity to the prospect of working with her.

I dove into the pool, the cool water refreshing against my hot skin. As I swam laps, my mind circled back to how she held her ground and challenged me. Not many people in my life have done that. I was eager to see where this would lead, and I knew one thing for sure: Kansas would bring a new and unexpected dynamic into my life.

The future looked far more interesting than it had in a long time.

Chapter 5:

Kansas

I threw a second pair of sandals into the suitcase with more force than necessary, grumbling under my breath. "I swear, I can't believe I let myself get roped into something like this. Writing a biography for *Dawson Lancaster*? I must be mentally challenged!"

Sitting on my desk chair, Mindy looked up from the book she was reading and adjusted her glasses with a knowing look. "Kansas, you know this is a good opportunity. You've been wanting to move out, and this job will give you the funds to do that."

I huffed, rifling through my closet for another outfit. "Yeah, but at what cost? Dawson Lancaster is the epitome of everything I despise. He's arrogant, entitled, and so out of touch with reality. He probably thinks poverty is just a character-building exercise."

Alyssa, sitting cross-legged on my bed, frowned. "Maybe he's just misunderstood. Not every rich person is bad, Kansas."

I paused, glancing at her. "Alyssa, this guy is a textbook case of privilege gone wrong. He's never had to work for anything in his life. Meanwhile, here we are, still living in this house, practically stumbling over each other."

Mindy sighed, closing her book. "Kansas, this is your chance to move on, to get the privacy you've been craving. Just try not to let your feelings cloud your judgment."

I tossed another dress into the suitcase. "Feelings? The only feeling I have toward Dawson Lancaster is disgust. The man's got a permanent smirk like he knows he's better than everyone else."

Alyssa reached over and squeezed my hand. "Just remember, you're doing this for yourself and us, not for him."

I managed a small smile. "You're right. I'll get through this, but I'm not promising I won't hate every minute of it."

Mindy shook her head, a hint of a smile on her lips. "Just try to keep an open mind, Kansas. You might be surprised."

"Doubt it," I muttered, zipping up the suitcase with a sense of finality. "But here goes nothing."

***

A few hours later, Shellene and I sat outside at our favorite little café, the sun warm on our shoulders as we sipped iced tea. The breeze carried the scent of the ocean, but even that couldn't soothe the irritation bubbling inside me.

"You're moving in with *Dawson Lancaster*?" Shellene asked, her eyes wide with awe and excitement.

I rolled my eyes, poking at my chicken pasta salad with a fork. "Yes, but it's not like I had a choice. It's the only way he'd agree to let me write his biography. He insists I need to 'immerse' myself in his life."

Shellene leaned in, her tone teasing. "Kansas, you're going to be living in the lap of luxury! A mansion, private chefs, the whole nine yards. And let's not forget—he's drop-dead gorgeous."

I scoffed, taking a sip of my tea. "Gorgeous, maybe. But he's also insufferable. He's arrogant, entitled, and thinks his money makes him better than everyone else."

Shellene laughed softly, shaking her head. "You don't know that for sure, and you're missing the point. You get to live in luxury and work on your own terms. Who cares if he's a little full of himself?"

I set my fork down and looked at her. "Shellene, it's not just about the money or the luxury. It's about being around someone who represents everything I can't stand. Dawson Lancaster has no idea what it's like to struggle, to really work for something."

She reached across the table and took my hand. "I get it, Kansas, I do. But maybe this is your chance to turn things around and finally get the space you've been craving. You don't have to like the guy to get what you want."

I sighed, leaning back in my chair. "Maybe you're right. But I just can't shake the feeling that living with him will be more trouble than it's worth."

Shellene smiled, her eyes twinkling with mischief. "Trouble isn't always a *bad* thing, you know. Sometimes, it leads to the best stories."

I chuckled despite myself. "We'll see about that. For now, I'm just focusing on surviving the duration."

Shellene raised her glass in a mock toast. "To surviving—and maybe even thriving."

I clinked my glass against hers, but deep down, I couldn't shake the feeling that this arrangement with Dawson would be anything *but* smooth sailing.

***

I had barely set foot in the mansion when the low, ominous growl reached my ears. My heart stopped, and I froze. Two Dobermans, their sleek, muscular bodies poised like predators, stood at the top of the grand staircase. Their dark eyes were fixed on me, and my breath caught in my throat as a wave of fear surged through me.

"Ah, I see you've met Nika and Loki," Dawson's voice drawled from behind me, laced with amusement. I didn't have to turn around to know he was smirking. The man took far too much pleasure in other people's discomfort.

I forced myself to step back, but my feet felt like lead. The memories of my childhood encounters with dogs, both times ending in bites and terror, flooded back with a vengeance. My pulse quickened, and I could feel the blood draining from my face.

"Relax," Dawson said, stepping beside me. His tone was casual as if we were discussing the weather and not the pair of terrifying beasts in front of us. "They're harmless unless you give them a reason not to be."

"Very comforting," I muttered, my voice shaky despite my attempt at sarcasm.

Dawson chuckled, clearly enjoying this. "You're afraid of dogs, aren't you?"

I shot him a glare, trying to mask my fear with anger. "What gave it away? The look of sheer terror on my face?"

He ignored my sarcasm and crouched, clicking his tongue to call the dogs over. To my horror, they obediently trotted down the stairs, their eyes never leaving me. I instinctively stepped back, practically scaling the wall to get further away from them, but Dawson reached out, catching my arm, which set my skin on fire.

"Hey," he said softly, his touch surprisingly gentle. "They're sweethearts, I promise."

Before I could protest, Nika was by my side, sniffing my hand. I froze, staring at the animal like it was a monster ready to eat me, but Dawson's grip on my arm kept me from pulling away. Loki, the larger of the two, stood next to Dawson, watching me with an unnerving intensity. Dawson rubbed Loki's head, his fingers threading through the dog's fur with ease, making it look almost affectionate.

"Try petting her," he suggested, his voice still soft. "Let her smell your hand first."

I shot him a look that could have melted steel. "You've got to be kidding me."

"Trust me," he said, his eyes meeting mine with an intensity that made my breath catch for an entirely different reason. "Nika won't hurt you. She just wants to say hello."

My heart pounded in my chest, but something in his gaze made me relax a tiny bit. I extended my hand slowly and against every instinct screaming at me to run for my life. Nika's nose was cold as it brushed against my skin, and then, to my utter shock, she licked my palm.

"She likes you," Dawson said, a note of triumph in his voice.

I swallowed hard, relief and disbelief washing over me. "I'm not sure that's a good thing."

Dawson laughed, the sound rich and warm, and, for a moment, it was disarming. "Come on, I'll show you to your suite."

Both dogs trotted beside Dawson as he took me through it. I was happy they were in front of me so I could keep my eye on them. Every once in a while, the bigger one—I was sure Dawson said his name was Loki—glanced over his shoulder. I wasn't convinced he didn't see me as food yet.

As he led me through the mansion, my mind raced, trying to process the fact that I would be living there. The mansion was stunning—no surprise there—filled with expensive art and tasteful décor that screamed wealth. It was the kind of place I'd always imagined people like Dawson lived in, surrounded by luxury and excess.

We walked down a long corridor, and every so often, his arm would brush against mine. Each time it happened, I'd jerk away, but the warmth from the contact lingered, making my skin tingle. It was infuriating how my body seemed to betray me.

When we reached the suite, Dawson pushed open the door with a flourish. "Here we are, your new home away from home."

I stepped inside and gasped. The room—no, *the suite*—was enormous, with a sitting area, a balcony overlooking the gardens, and a bed that looked like it could fit a small army. It was the epitome of luxury, and I felt a pang of guilt just standing in it.

"This is too much," I said, turning to him. "Do you have anything smaller?"

Dawson laughed, then shrugged, leaning against the door frame with that infuriatingly smug smile. "Only the best for my biographer. Besides, you'll be staying here for a while. Might as well get comfortable."

"Comfortable," I echoed, unable to keep the skepticism out of my voice. "Right."

He stepped closer, his gaze locking onto mine. For a moment, I actually thought he might kiss me. He was so close that I felt his hot breath when he exhaled. The air between us thickened, charged with something I didn't want to name. My heart raced, and I hated that he could make me feel this way—vulnerable, exposed.

But then, just as quickly, he pulled back, a smirk playing on his lips.

And with that, he turned and left, leaving me standing there, my emotions a tangled mess. I stared at the door for a long moment, my heart still pounding, wondering what the hell I had gotten myself into.

As I settled into the plush armchair in my suite, trying to catch my breath from the whirlwind that was Dawson Lancaster, a knock sounded at the door. Before I could answer, Dawson strolled in like he owned the place— which, of course, he did.

"Dinner's at seven," he said, his tone casual, but his eyes locked onto mine with that same authoritative glint. "Don't be late."

"I think I'll pass," I replied, keeping my voice steady, though the undercurrent of tension between us was undeniable.

He raised an eyebrow, his lips curving into a smirk. "That wasn't a request, Kansas."

I stood, meeting his gaze head-on. "You can't just tell me what to do, Dawson. I'm not one of your employees."

He took a step closer, his expression hardening. "I can send you home anytime I see fit. It would do you well to remember that."

Fury bubbled up inside me, and I couldn't hold it back. "You think you can just control everyone around you, don't you, Mr. High & Mighty? Well, not me!"

Dawson paused, his eyes narrowing slightly. "Is that your decision, then? Because this is who I am. You can take it or leave it."

My heart pounded in my chest, but I refused to back down. "Fine. I'll be there, but only because I'm hungry."

"Good," he said, a faint smile returning. "I'll see you promptly at seven."

I took a deep breath before stepping into the dining room, 10 minutes past seven. Dawson was already seated at the head of the table, his expression unreadable, but his eyes flicked to the clock as I entered.

"You're late," he said, his tone measured, though I could sense the edge beneath it.

"I planned it that way," I replied, lifting my chin defiantly.

Silence hung between us for a moment, then Dawson chuckled, the sound low and unexpectedly warm. "Touché," he said, leaning back in his chair. "Let's call it a truce, then."

Surprised, I blinked at him. "A truce?"

He nodded. "We got off on the wrong foot. Let's start over."

I hesitated, then slowly nodded. "Alright. I can agree to that."

The tension in the room eased a fraction as he gestured for me to sit. "Not as bad as you thought it would be?" he asked, a hint of amusement in his voice.

I smirked slightly, sitting down across from him. "Not yet, anyway."

He smiled, and for the first time, it felt genuine. We shared bits of personal information as the dinner progressed—nothing too deep, just enough to ease the silence. But even as we talked, I couldn't ignore how his mere presence seemed to heat the air between us. Every glance and word seemed charged with something I wasn't ready to name.

Dawson must have felt it, too, because every so often, his gaze would linger on me a moment longer than necessary. I forced myself to focus on the conversation, determined not to let him see how much he affected me.

"Let's see how long this truce lasts," I said, more to myself than to him.

He smiled again, and for a moment, I wondered if maybe this wouldn't be as terrible as I'd imagined. But I couldn't shake the feeling that this was only the beginning of a much more complicated story.

After dinner, Dawson walked me up the stairs. As we reached my suite, Dawson turned to me, a wicked glint in his eyes. "So, Kansas," he drawled, "will you be sleeping in your own bed tonight or mine?"

Fury ignited in my chest. "You arrogant, self-absorbed, insufferable—" I unleashed a string of names, each one more venomous than the last.

He whirled around, stepping closer until I was pressed against the wall. His arms caged me in, his lips just inches from mine. I took a shaky breath, mortified that a tiny part of me wanted him to kiss me.

He didn't kiss me, of course. Instead, he said, "Don't worry, you'll find yourself in my bed at some point; most women do."

"Dawson Lancaster!. You will not lay one hand on me, you jerk!" I pushed him away, turned on my heel, and opened the door to my room.

"Good night, Kansas. Sleep tight," I heard him say after I slammed the door shut, rage flowing through my veins.

I muttered profanities the entire time I ran my bath, but when I immersed myself in the luxurious spa tub, a sense of calm helped soothe my nerves.

I considered leaving, but I really needed the two hundred thousand dollars. All the same, I was *not* going to let the likes of Dawson Lancaster get to me like that again, and he'd better stop messing with me if he knew what was good for him!

Chapter 6:

Dawson

I woke up before dawn, lying in the quiet stillness of the morning. The first thought that came to mind was Kansas, fast asleep in the guest room down the hall. I wondered if I should wake her up. I glanced at the clock. No, I should let her sleep. After all, I knew what it was like sleeping in a new bed—adjusting would take a night or two. Though considering the king-sized, top-of-the-line mattress I gave her, it would be hard to imagine she had anything *but* sweet dreams.

I slid out of bed, threw on some swim trunks, and headed outside. Loki and Nika bounded toward me, tails wagging, their sleek black and tan bodies cutting through the early morning mist. "Alright, alright, settle down," I muttered, giving each a pat before diving into the pool. The water was cool and refreshing and gave me a moment to think. Loki jumped in after me, but Nika kept pacing around the pool's edge in protection mode.

"Nika, I'm fine, girl. Relax." I told her and walked to the edge. Nika nuzzled my hand, and I picked her up and brought her into the pool. Once immersed in the water, she chased Loki while I watched in amusement. It was never dull with them around.

I swam a few laps and then rested to watch them again, Kansas coming into my mind. I chuckled, thinking about the last thing I'd asked her before she practically fled to bed. Did she really believe I was serious about her sleeping in my bed? It had been worth it just to see her reaction—eyes wide, stammering. Maybe I'd tease her about it later. After all, if we were working this closely, a little fun was inevitable.

***

I was lounging by the pool, sipping freshly squeezed orange juice, the sun already warming the Miami air. Loki and Nika were stretched out beside me on their comfy outdoor beds, enjoying the morning as much as I was. I glanced at my watch—it was almost noon. I figured Kansas should be up soon, but I wasn't in any hurry.

Suddenly, the glass door slid open with a sharp **swish**, and there she was, storming out in a flurry of frustration. Her messy hair and narrowed eyes told me everything I needed to know.

"Dawson, it's almost **noon**!" She dragged out the word 'noon' like a wailing teenager. "Why didn't you wake me up?" Her voice was high-pitched and tight, bordering on furious. *Yep, definitively like a spoiled brat teenager!*

I didn't even bother sitting up—I just glanced at her with a raised brow. "It's not my job to wake you up, Kansas. I figured you could use the sleep."

She folded her arms, clearly not satisfied with that answer. "I like to get up early and get a head start on my day. I could have been working for hours by now."

I chuckled, taking another sip of my juice before responding. "Well, hate to break it to you, but getting up early isn't going to help you much around here. I like to sleep in most days. Today is different because I had an early Zoom call. There will be many nights where we'll work late, probably into the wee hours of the morning, so you'll need to be well-rested."

Her eyes flared. "Don't try to control my sleeping schedule, Dawson. I'm here to work, not to lounge around like some trophy," she spat.

I shrugged, more amused by her indignation than anything. "Not trying to control anything. Just saying, if you're going to work with me, you'll have to get used to my pace." I waved a hand, and almost as if on cue, my chef appeared, wheeling out a silver tray piled high with breakfast. Eggs Benedict, fresh fruit, pancakes, you name it—it was all there, and it smelled divine.

"Here's breakfast. Come sit. Eat. Relax. It's a beautiful day. I'm just going to hang by the pool for a bit. You should join me."

Her face turned red, clearly not impressed with my offer. "When are we going to start *working*?" Her frustration was noticeable.

I leaned back into the lounge chair and closed my eyes, the sunlight hitting my face perfectly. "I don't feel like working yet. Too nice outside. Why rush it?"

She huffed, clearly on the verge of losing her patience. "Dawson, this is ridiculous. We have a lot to get started, and I don't have time to waste."

I cracked an eye open. "Kansas, the world isn't going to end because we start a little late. Take a breath and eat. Stop worrying about hurrying through this in order to get your money."

Her jaw dropped, and I had to fight my laughter. "You've got to be kidding me. I'm not doing that, but I'm here to do a job, not laze around by the pool all day."

I shrugged. "Suit yourself, but I'm going to have some delicious breakfast and get back to my hectic day lounging around the pool. It would be most enjoyable if you joined me."

After breakfast, I could see the frustration building in Kansas as she sat stiffly by the pool, her arms crossed and eyes glaring at me. She wasn't saying it out loud, but I knew what was on her mind—she just wanted to write the damn book and go home. And because of that, I decided to take my time.

I stood, stretching lazily before diving into the pool. The cool water was perfect, but it was even better knowing it would drive her crazy. I surfaced and looked over at her. "Come on, Kansas. Join me. It'll do you some good."

She shook her head firmly. "No. We have work to do, so let's get to it."

I swam toward the edge, watching her tense as I approached. With a grin, I reached up, grabbed her by the waist, and pulled her into the water. Her startled scream echoed through the backyard as she splashed beside me.

"Dawson! What the *hell*!" she shouted, water dripping down her face.

"You needed to cool off," I said with a laugh, wrapping my arms around her waist. That's when I realized it—she was pressed tightly against me, and the electricity between us was undeniable. I could feel her body, every single curve, and I knew she felt it too.

Her eyes widened slightly, and we locked gazes. Everything inside me screamed to lean down and kiss her and close the distance. I pulled her tighter, our breath mingling, but at the last second, I fought the urge. Instead, I did the next best thing.

With a grin, I lifted her and tossed her across the pool. She gasped as she hit the water, coming up sputtering and furious.

"You're insufferable!" she snapped, splashing water at me.

I just laughed, already planning my next move.

Kansas was fuming, her cheeks flushed with anger, but I couldn't help the grin tugging at my lips. I swam lazily in the pool, ignoring her fury.

"How about this," I said, pushing off the wall and gliding through the water toward her, "let's settle it with a race. I'll throw in another $100,000 to your pay if you win."

Her eyes widened, and she glared at me, disbelief and fury flashing across her face. "You're ridiculous," she snapped.

I chuckled. "Maybe. But it'll be fun. So, what do you say? I'll even let you push off before I start." I grinned, knowing that she couldn't resist a challenge.

"You're on," she finally said, her voice tight with determination.

We lined up at one end of the pool. "On three," I said, "One... two... three!" She shot off like a rocket, and true to my word, I waited until she was finished before I pushed off. Kansas was fast, but I was quicker. When I touched the far wall, I knew I'd won. I surfaced with a smug grin, watching her arrive a moment later, her face a mask of frustration.

"Too bad," I teased, "You just lost $100,000."

Her face turned red with anger. "You don't get it, do you? You just toss your money around like it's a baseball. Meanwhile, people like me have had to fight for everything we have. You think this is just a game." she shot back.

I shrugged, my tone light but pointed. "Interesting. You had no problem with the money when you had a chance of winning it. Now that you've lost, suddenly I'm the bad guy."

Kansas huffed and clenched her fists, refusing to look at me. Her silence said everything. I smirked, knowing I'd hit a nerve. This woman was full of fire, and I couldn't help but be even more intrigued.

Kansas climbed out of the pool, water dripping off her, and shot me a glare as she reached for a towel. "We need to start working, Dawson."

I leaned back, grinning. "Chill, Kansas. Meet me for dinner, and we'll work this evening."

She huffed, hands on her hips. "I'm serious."

"So am I."

***

Kansas showed up for dinner, still looking annoyed, but I could tell she was trying to mask it with professionalism. She sat down, eying the gourmet spread before quickly shifting her gaze to me.

"We need to focus on the book," she said, attempting to steer the conversation. "Tell me about your upbringing. What shaped you into this role you now play?"

I smirked and leaned back in my chair. "For every question you answer about yourself, I'll answer one for you. Deal?"

She hesitated, but nodded. "Fine. Ask."

I raised an eyebrow, amused. "What's your favorite thing to write about?"

Her eyes flickered with surprise, but she answered, "Animals. They're honest and uncomplicated."

I nodded. "Alright. As for me, my mother shaped a lot of who I am. She's determined to a fault."

Kansas pressed on. "Why did you start Lancaster Luxury Estates?"

I tilted my head and grinned. "Why do you hate the rich?"

Her lips pressed together tightly, clearly not expecting that. "I don't *hate* the rich; I just grew up seeing what greed does to people."

I smiled slightly. "Interesting." The questions continued, becoming more personal with each turn. Finally, I leaned in, lowering my voice. "Have you ever been in love, Kansas?"

She blinked, caught off guard. The silence hung heavy between us.

"I am not going to answer that. That has nothing to do with—"

"Shh. You don't have to answer that right now. I'll leave it with you, but I want an answer tomorrow *before* we start working." I narrowed my eyes to let her know I meant what I said.

Kansas stood abruptly, glaring at me. "Come find me when you're serious and ready to work on your book," she snapped, then stormed off.

I leaned back in my chair, watching her go. My eyes trailed after her, appreciating the sway of her hips.

What a beautiful rump, I thought with a grin, shaking my head in amusement.

She was fiery, no doubt about that. It would be fun getting under her skin, but she didn't realize I always played by my own rules.

I'd find her when I was ready.

Chapter 7:

Kansas

I woke up to the bright sun filtering through my curtains, my internal alarm clock pulling me from sleep right on time—8 a.m. A glance at the clock confirmed it. As much as I dreaded the thought, I knew I'd have to deal with Dawson at some point today, but it was still early. Knowing him, he wouldn't be up for hours.

I grabbed my phone and called Shellene. If anyone could get my mind off that irritating man, it was her.

"Breakfast?" I asked as soon as she picked up.

"Always," she replied with a laugh. "Meet me at Bennett's Bistro?"

Twenty minutes later, I sat across from her at a small table outside, the warm summer air of Miami already beginning to creep in.

"So," Shellene began, grinning as she sipped her iced coffee, "how's it going with Mr. Fancy-Pants?"

I groaned, rolling my eyes. "Don't get me started on Dawson. He's the most infuriating, arrogant—"

"Oh, please," she interrupted, laughing. "You've been talking about him non-stop since we sat down. I think you might be more interested in him than you're letting on."

I snorted. "I'm only talking about him because he's so irritating. I need to vent, or I'll explode."

Shellene leaned in, eyes twinkling with mischief. "Uh-huh. Or maybe you're just attracted to him."

I nearly choked on my coffee. "What? No way! He's the last person on earth I'd ever be attracted to."

"Sure, sure," she teased. "But you've spent this entire meal talking about him."

I sighed. "It's because he's such a jerk. Rich, entitled. Ugh, reminds me of Tripp Farragher."

"Tripp?" Shellene raised an eyebrow. "You mean the fireman who left you for one of your best friends?"

"Yeah. I swear, men can't be trusted."

"Dawson isn't Tripp," she pointed out.

"Maybe not," I muttered, "but they're all the same. You can't trust any of them."

Shellene smiled, her voice softening. "Not all men are the same, Kansas. There are some good ones out there, real treasures. I'm still holding out for my knight in shining armor."

I shook my head, laughing. "Good luck with that."

Just as I finished laughing with Shellene, my phone buzzed. It was a text from Dawson.

Dawson: Where are you?

Dawson: I thought we could work this afternoon.

Dawson: Since it's supposed to rain.

I rolled my eyes. "He's such a big baby," I muttered, showing Shellene the message. "I'm thinking of shopping and then catching a movie, just to make him wait."

Shellene shook her head. "Don't push your luck. You don't want to mess with losing the job."

I huffed. "He'll survive without me for one afternoon."

Shellene grinned. "True, but can you survive without that paycheck?"

I sighed. "Ugh, fine. I'm going. He's so demanding."

"That's because he's used to getting his way," she said, smirking. "Now, go on, face the music."

Reluctantly, I stood up.

***

The sky darkened as I pulled up to Dawson's mansion, the first fat raindrops splattering against my windshield—a typical Miami summer storm. I sighed, reluctant to head inside. Dawson had texted me hours ago, but I wasn't in a rush to deal with him. Not today. Yet, here I was, pulling myself out of the car as the rain began to pour in earnest.

I dashed toward the massive outdoor gazebo, spotting him lounging there with a spread of journals laid out in front of him, utterly unfazed by the storm.

"What on earth are you doing out here?" I called as I stepped into the shelter of the gazebo, brushing raindrops off my arms.

Dawson didn't even glance up. "Working," he replied coolly, as though it were perfectly normal to be sitting outside in the middle of a thunderstorm. His sharp blue eyes flicked over to me, but he said nothing about the fact that I'd been gone most of the day.

I sat down across from him, pulling a journal toward me. "So, how are we structuring this thing?" I asked, trying to sound more professional than I felt. I still couldn't get used to the fact that I was writing a biography for someone like him. Someone I couldn't stand.

"I want to work backward," Dawson said, flipping through another journal. "Start with the empire I've built and touch on my childhood last."

I frowned, looking up at him. "That's unusual. Most people would start with their upbringing, build a foundation."

He shrugged, his eyes narrowing slightly. "I'm not 'most people.' My childhood isn't the foundation of who I am today. At least, not in the way you might think."

There was a strange look in his eyes when he mentioned his childhood, a flicker of something I couldn't quite place. Pain? Bitterness? Either way, I wasn't about to pry. At least, not yet. I simply nodded. "Alright. Backward it is."

We dove into the work, reviewing the timeline and noting the significant events Dawson wanted to highlight. His rise to power, the hotels, and the significant acquisitions. But as the storm outside grew more intense, I found myself glancing out nervously. Every crack of thunder made me jump in my seat, though I tried to hide it.

Of course, Dawson noticed. "You're not afraid of a little thunder, are you?"

I bristled. "No, of course not. It's just loud, that's all."

His lips quirked into a grin, but he didn't press further. The rain suddenly shifted, now coming in sideways. Water sprayed in from the open sides of the gazebo. Afraid it would drench the journals, I picked them up and set them on the little table behind me where the rain couldn't reach.

"Great," Dawson muttered, grabbing the papers before him. "Let's move to the back."

We scrambled to the narrow corner of the gazebo, huddling under the small roof where the rain couldn't reach. There wasn't much room, and before I knew it, my back was pressed against Dawson's front. My breath hitched.

Neither of us moved.

I could feel the warmth of his chest against me, his breath on the back of my neck, and every nerve in my body went on high alert. The storm roared around us, but all I could hear was the sound of his steady and calm breathing.

"Are you cold?" His voice was low, almost too close.

I stiffened. "No."

But then my body shivered, betraying my lie. Without hesitation, Dawson's arms slid around me, pulling me close.

I froze. "What are you doing?"

"Trying to keep you warm," he said simply, his voice genuine. "Relax."

But how could I relax with his hard body pressed against mine? The feel of him was too much, too intense. Heat rushed to my cheeks, and I suddenly felt like I couldn't breathe. I had to get out of here.

Without thinking, I bolted right into the storm.

"Kansas!" Dawson shouted after me, but I didn't stop. I sprinted through the rain, slipping on the slick grass, my heart racing.

Then my foot caught on something, and I went down hard. The wind was knocked out of me, and the next thing I knew, Dawson was there, lifting me in his arms like I weighed nothing.

"Stop running," he growled, carrying me back toward the house.

"I wasn't—" I started to protest, but he cut me off.

"You're going to hurt yourself."

We reached the kitchen, and Dawson set me down gently before grabbing a small towel. He started drying me off, but it was ridiculous—his large hands and the tiny towel barely made a dent in the soaking mess I was.

I couldn't help it. I burst out laughing. "Are you serious?" I giggled, wiping water from my face. "That's not helping."

Dawson joined in, a low chuckle rumbling through his chest. "You're right. Here." He made a halfhearted attempt to dry my arms, but we both knew it was futile.

Our laughter filled the room, and for a moment, the tension between us disappeared. But then, without warning, Dawson grabbed me, pulling me close, his eyes darkening. Before I could react, his lips crashed down on mine.

The kiss was fierce, filled with a heat and hunger that caught me off guard. I found myself responding for a second, my body betraying me as I melted into him.

But then reality hit me like a bucket of cold water. I pushed him away, my heart racing.

"What the hell was that?" I demanded, glaring at him.

Dawson blinked, confused. "I—"

"You took advantage of the situation!" I snapped, stepping back. "I'm not some conquest, Dawson."

He frowned, his expression hardening. "That wasn't my intention."

"Well, it sure felt like it."

With that, I stormed off, the heat of the kiss still lingering on my lips, even as my mind screamed that I needed to stay far, far away from him.

I sat on the edge of the bed, pulling up Zoom on my laptop. My heart was already lighter at the thought of seeing Mindy and Alyssa's faces. The familiar sound of the call connecting brought a smile.

"There she is!" Alyssa's bright voice greeted me as her face popped onto the screen.

"Kansas, you look tired," Mindy chimed in, her wise, ever-observant gaze piercing through the screen.

I sighed. "I miss you guys. I just want to come home."

Alyssa frowned. "You're not thinking of quitting, are you? We need you to finish that book—it'll benefit all of us. Just remember, it's only temporary."

Mindy nodded in agreement. "You've got this, Kansas. Besides, imagine what selling this story could do for your career."

They were right, of course, but it didn't make staying here any easier. "I know, but working for Dawson is exhausting."

Alyssa leaned in closer to the camera, her eyes wide with curiosity. "What's it like working for a billionaire?"

I hesitated, biting my lip. The memory of that kiss flashed in my mind, the heat of it still lingering on my lips. "It certainly is interesting," I said, trying to sound casual. "He's demanding, a total control freak. But he knows what he wants."

Mindy raised an eyebrow. "That's all?"

"Yeah," I replied quickly, deliberately leaving out the fiery kiss that had me all twisted up inside. "That's all."

Alyssa smiled. "You're doing amazing, Kansas. Just hang in there."

"I'm trying," I said, forcing a smile. "I should go. I love you both, and I'll see you soon."

I hung up, my fingers grazing my lips as the lingering warmth from Dawson's kiss flared back to life. But I wasn't ready to admit that—especially not to myself.

I lay in bed, staring at the ceiling, unable to sleep. My mind was racing—Dawson, the book, the kiss. I groaned and threw the blanket off, knowing there was no way I'd be getting any rest tonight.

I slipped out of bed and wandered through the quiet mansion. Despite my initial reluctance, I had to admit—

I loved this place: the high ceilings, the elegant decor, the sheer luxury of it all. I found myself in the kitchen and was about to grab some water when I noticed movement outside.

Dawson was in the pool.

Curious, I tiptoed closer, standing by the glass doors, watching him glide through the water effortlessly. Something about seeing him like this, so relaxed, caught me off guard. I debated joining him, but he got out of the pool before I could decide.

And he was completely naked!

My heart jumped into my throat, and I couldn't stop staring. Every inch of him was on display, and my mind short-circuited. Oh my God!

Realizing what I was doing, I spun around and hurried back to my room, my heart hammering in my chest. But when I finally crawled back into bed, all I could think about was Dawson, and my dreams were filled with him—sexy, dangerous, and impossible to ignore.

Chapter 8:

Dawson

I tossed my phone on the table and turned to Kansas, who was seated on the couch, glaring at me like I'd just ruined her day—which, I suppose, I had.

"We're leaving for Iceland this afternoon," I said, keeping my tone casual. I braced myself for her reaction.

She blinked, her eyes narrowing. "What? You're joking, right? You didn't even tell me."

"It's last minute," I replied, shrugging. "But I need you to pack. We're touring a few of my hotels—different countries, different continents. We'll be gone for a while."

Kansas crossed her arms, disbelief written across her face. "I can't just leave right now."

I grinned, leaning against the doorway. "Why not? What else do you have on your schedule today?"

She shot me a look that could melt glass. "We're supposed to be working on your book," she reminded me.

"We'll have plenty of time for that en-route." I winked.

She sighed, her fingers fidgeting with the edge of her notebook. "I've never seen snow up close. How cold is it there?"

"Cold," I said, "but don't worry. I'll keep you warm."

Her glare could have frozen me in place. "You're impossible."

"I'm teasing." I raised my hands in surrender. "I'll even help you pack."

***

As I helped her gather her things an hour later, our hands brushed several times, each touch sending an unexpected jolt of electricity. We locked eyes, her lips parting, but the moment passed.

"Stop grinning like that," she muttered.

"I can't help it," I said, smirking. "You're fun to mess with."

She shoved a sweater into her bag. "This trip is going to be a nightmare. I can't believe you expect me to just up and leave like this with no warning."

"Oh, you'll love it," I said. "You just don't know it yet. I'm sorry; this is my life. Things come up last minute all the time."

She groaned. "Very funny. I think you just want to torture me. Why don't you go by yourself? I'll just have a little mini vacation here? We can continue when you get back."

She looked so hopeful. "Don't be like that. You need to let loose a little and have some fun."

She smirked, "I can do that just fine while you're gone."

"I'll bet you can," I said, grabbing her suitcase.

"You're such a gentleman. I can carry it by myself, you know."

"Oh, I'm sure you can, but this way, I don't have to hear all your whining and complaining. Grab your passport— the limo is waiting," I told her as I descended the stairs. I walked outside to where Gilbert, our driver, was leaning against the white limo. Gilbert tipped his hat at me and grinned. "Where to today?"

"The airport. Off to Ireland." Gilbert nodded and took the suitcase. He turned to Kansas as I introduced them.

"You're a lucky one, miss. You'll get to see the Northern Lights in Ireland. Such a breathtaking sight."

Kansas looked at me and asked, "Will we have time for that?"

"Of course. I have time for anything. I make my own schedule," I reminded her with a laugh.

The drive to the airport was only 20 minutes long, and she was silent the entire time. "I'm sorry. I'm not trying to be rude, but I have to let my family know where I'll be." She seemed pretty preoccupied, but I didn't mind. It gave me a chance to watch her.

Kansas stopped dead in her tracks as we stepped onto my private jet. Her eyes doubled in size, her mouth slightly open, and she looked utterly speechless for the first time since we'd met. The child-like awe in her expression caught me off guard. I watched as her eyes darted around, taking in the sleek leather seats, the polished wood accents, and the spacious cabin. She was utterly enchanted.

"Wow," she breathed, almost reverently, trailing a hand along one of the seats. "This is unreal."

I couldn't help but smile. "You like it?"

She turned to me, still wide-eyed. "Like it? Dawson, this is insane. People *actually* fly like this?"

I chuckled, settling into one of the seats and motioning for her to do the same. "Well, not most people. Commercial planes are nothing like this. Welcome to the world of the ultra-rich," I teased, knowing she hated that term. Her glare was half-hearted at best; she was too caught up in the experience.

She sat down, sinking into the plush leather with an audible sigh. I could see her trying to compose herself, but the excitement bubbling just beneath the surface was undeniable. There was something about seeing Kansas like this—unguarded, full of wonder—that was oddly captivating. I found myself watching her more closely than I meant to.

As the jet took off, she gripped the armrests, her knuckles turning white. But as soon as we were in the air, her frown melted away, and she leaned forward, peering out the window with a look of pure joy.

"I think I love flying," she said, her voice filled with quiet amazement.

I raised an eyebrow, unable to suppress my grin. "You've never flown before? I find that hard to believe."

Kansas shook her head, still glued to the window. "Nope. It just never came up."

"Never came up?" I echoed, leaning back in my seat. "What a shame. You've really been missing out."

She turned to face me, her usual fire returning. "Not *all* of us have private jets, Dawson. Some of us have to live in the real world."

I shrugged, enjoying the banter. "Well, now you're not missing out anymore, are you?"

She huffed, but I could tell she was enjoying herself.

I watched her for a long moment, more intrigued than I cared to admit. Kansas was something else—stubborn, sure, but also passionate and creative. Watching her discover the thrill of flying for the first time was simply enchanting.

As we stepped out of the car, the biting cold hit us immediately, a sharp contrast to the Miami heat we'd left behind. The streets were blanketed in snow, the ice glittering like diamonds under the pale moonlight. Kansas stood still momentarily, her breath visible in the frosty air. I watched her eyes wide as they took in the landscape.

"Wow," she whispered, her voice almost lost in the stillness. "It's like something out of a dream."

I smiled, watching her. There was something magical about seeing her experience this for the first time—the way the snow crunched under her boots and the soft awe in her eyes. "Welcome to Lancaster Luxury Estates, Iceland."

Her gaze flicked to me, a touch of disbelief still lingering. "It's incredible. I've never seen anything like it."

"Iceland has that effect on people." I gestured toward the towering hotel ahead, its sleek glass walls reflecting the ice and sky. "Come on, I'll introduce you to my manager, Thad Nixxon."

Inside, the warmth was immediate. I always ensured the temperature in my hotels was perfect to make my guests feel comfortable. We made our way to Thad's office on the 22nd floor. Thad greeted us with a firm handshake, his smile wide.

"Ms. Stonehouse," Thad said, "it's a pleasure to meet you. Dawson's told me you'll be working closely together." Thad was probably the best-dressed man in my hotel—a silvery gray suit that matched his salt and pepper hair and a burgundy silk dress shirt and handkerchief in the pocket. It was good to know I paid him well.

Kansas nodded, still a bit awestruck. "Nice to meet you, Mr. Nixxon."

Thad's light gray eyes filled with delight as he said, "The pleasure is surely mine." He turned to me and said, "I had your chef prepare a nice light late-night meal for you. I'm sure you're exhausted and starving." I nodded my approval.

After we ate and I introduced Kansas to some of the staff, I turned to Kansas. "Do you want to explore the grounds with me?"

She hesitated, glancing out at the snow-covered world beyond the windows. "Sure," she finally said, her voice laced with curiosity. "Why not?"

As we walked outside, her steps were cautious, but her wonder was unmistakable. "I wasn't prepared for how beautiful it would be," she said quietly, her breath fogging up in the cold. "Or how cold." She shivered and wrapped her arms around herself.

"Don't worry," I teased, stepping closer. "I'll keep you warm."

She shot me a glare, but I could see the corners of her mouth twitching. "Keep your hands to yourself."

"Maybe." I chuckled. "But you're starting to enjoy this, aren't you? Let's walk some more. I want to show you something special."

"What is it?" she asked breathlessly as she tried to keep up with me.

The path ahead of us was straight out of a winter fairytale. Colorful lights hung from snow-covered trees, and little campfires dotted the path, their flames flickering and crackling in the still air. Every so often, there were huts offering hot chocolate and apple cider, the sweet scents mixing with the crisp air. Snow fell lightly around us, adding to the magic of the moment.

Kansas walked beside me, her wide-eyed wonder evident as she took it all in. "This is a winter wonderland if I ever saw one," she whispered, her breath fogging up in the cold.

I smiled to myself, enjoying the way she seemed enchanted by everything. It was rare to see her this unguarded.

Suddenly, her foot slipped on a patch of black ice. Before she could hit the ground, I caught her, pulling her tight against me. My arm wrapped around her waist instinctively, her body pressed against mine.

"Careful," I murmured, but I didn't let go. Something about the way the snow fell around us, her soft gasp, made it impossible to resist. I leaned in slowly and pressed my lips to hers. The kiss was slow and sensual, and for a moment, everything else disappeared.

I could feel her hesitation after a moment, and before she could pull away, I broke the kiss first, letting the cold air rush back between us. She looked up at me, her expression unreadable.

Without a word, I reached for her hand and held it tightly. "Can't have you slipping again," I said softly, my voice low.

She didn't argue, and we continued walking in silence, the snow crunching under our boots. I kept her hand in mine, and I could feel the heat transfer between us.

***

I called Kansas to my room an hour later, and she showed up, looking a little wary but professional. We sat by the fireplace, the warmth crackling in the air as we reviewed some notes for the biography. I poured us both a glass of red wine, and the atmosphere quickly became more relaxed as the late evening hours wore on.

She leaned back in her chair, her fingers loosely holding her glass as we finished the last bit of work. "Not bad," she said, glancing at the pages. "You actually make a decent subject."

I smirked. "High praise coming from you."

When we were done, I set the notes aside and looked at her. "You want to stay for a nightcap?"

I saw her hesitate, which was evidence that she wanted to, but she shook her head and stood up. "No, thanks. I've had enough wine for tonight."

I didn't push it. Instead, I offered to walk her to her room. When we got to her door, an unease settled between us, and I looked at her curiously.

I couldn't resist. I leaned down and kissed her again, slow and deep. For a moment, she responded, her lips soft against mine, but then, abruptly, she pulled away.

"Goodnight, Dawson," she said, her voice firm, and disappeared into her room, leaving me standing in the hallway, stunned and wanting more.

Chapter 9:

Kansas

I woke up, the memory of last night replaying vividly. That kiss was something else. Had the wine muddled my judgment? One thing was for sure—it couldn't happen again. I was determined to steer clear of Dawson for the rest of the trip. No more alcohol!

I dressed, feeling odd in the winter clothes Dawson had so thoughtfully bought me: a hat, gloves, boots, and layers. The Miami sun never required such things, but he had said layering was the trick to staying warm.

Half an hour later, I was about to knock on Dawson's hotel door when it suddenly swung open.

"You're early," he said, flashing that infuriating grin.

I rolled my eyes.

When Dawson's eyes swept over my bundled form, he gave a satisfied nod. "You'll be warm enough," he remarked, his eyes lingering just a moment too long. Then, that infuriating smirk appeared. "I've got a surprise for you."

I wanted to groan, but curiosity tugged at me. I followed Dawson outside, the cold air biting at my face, even through the layers. We stepped out into the frozen landscape, and I blinked in astonishment. A Svalbard dog sled was waiting for us; the dogs yipped excitedly, their fur thick and bristling against the cold.

"Are you serious?" I asked, my voice betraying excitement *and* disbelief.

Dawson chuckled, clearly enjoying my reaction. "You'll love it. Trust me."

I wasn't sure if I could trust him, but the sight of the sled dogs and the idea of soaring over the ice piqued my interest enough to climb aboard. As soon as we settled, the dogs took off in a blur of energy, their paws barely skimming the snow as we glided across the vast, frozen wilderness.

The sled ride was magical and far more exhilarating than I could have imagined. The cold wind whipped at my face, but I barely felt it. The scenery entranced me—the stark white snow against the endless sky, the rhythmic thumping of the dogs' paws as they pulled us deeper into the wintry expanse. My breath fogged in the air as the sound of the sled runners slicing through the snow caught my attention. I swore I must be dreaming, and I felt free and weightless for the first time in a long while.

I couldn't help but smile. "This is incredible."

"I thought you'd like it," Dawson said from beside me, his voice warm though he was half-hidden beneath his layers of winter gear. "Just wait. The best part is still ahead."

I wasn't sure what could top this until we slowed and finally stopped before an imposing ice formation. Towering crystalline walls glistened in the pale light, casting shimmering blue hues. Dawson gestured toward the opening, and I hesitated momentarily before stepping inside the ice cave.

The air was colder and crisper. I could hear the faintest echo of our footsteps bouncing off the glistening walls. The ice seemed to glow from within, casting an ethereal light that danced across Dawson's face as he walked ahead. It was otherworldly—how the cavern sparkled, like something from a fairy tale. I reached out to touch one of the walls, feeling the cold seep into my fingers, but it was so smooth, like polished glass.

"Unreal," I whispered, my voice echoing softly around us.

Dawson turned, his smile more genuine this time. "Worth it?"

I nodded, too entranced to argue with him for once. The silence and beauty of the cave enveloped me, and for a fleeting moment, I forgot all about my complicated feelings toward him. It was just the ice, the quiet, and the shimmering magic of this hidden world.

But, of course, that moment didn't last.

As we walked deeper into the cave, I slipped on a patch of ice, my feet flying out from under me. Before I could catch myself, I hit the ground with a grunt. Dawson was at my side in an instant, offering his hand. His lips quirked into that arrogant grin I'd come to despise.

"You know," he drawled, "if you wanted me to catch you, you just had to ask."

My cheeks flamed with embarrassment and fury. "Oh, please," I snapped, batting his hand away as I struggled to get up. "Not everything revolves around you."

He laughed, the sound echoing off the icy walls. "You're right. But I'm still here to save you, whether you like it or not."

I huffed, refusing to meet his gaze as I brushed the ice off my pants. "I can handle myself."

"I'm sure you can," he teased, his voice softer this time. "But next time, maybe just don't try to do it on purpose."

I glared at him, fighting the urge to retaliate with a sharp comeback. But the truth was, the beauty of the ice cave had disarmed me. As much as I wanted to hate him, the magic of the moment made it harder to keep my walls intact. I turned my focus back to the glittering cave around us, vowing to stay on my feet from here on out—literally and figuratively.

On the ride back to the hotel, I couldn't stop talking. The caves were beyond anything I'd imagined—the way the ice shimmered, the colors dancing in the light, the quiet stillness that felt almost sacred. I was a little miss chatterbox, recounting every detail to Dawson, the excitement bubbling over.

"And did you see how the light just—oh, and that one tunnel with the—"

I caught sight of him smiling at me, clearly amused. I shut my mouth abruptly, cheeks burning. "What?" I snapped, crossing my arms.

Dawson chuckled, his laughter warm and teasing. "Nothing. You're just so dramatic. It's entertaining."

I huffed, but my embarrassment lingered. "I am not being dramatic; I'm just recounting the day's sights." I crossed my arms indignantly.

"Oh, of course. How could I have mixed that up?" He grinned.

Later, just before dinner, we decided to try the hot springs surrounding the hotel. The steam rising from the water created a soft haze as I slipped inside slowly, feeling the heat relax my muscles instantly. But it wasn't just the hot springs making me feel warm.

Dawson emerged from the changing room in his bathing suit, and I couldn't help but stare. His chiseled abs, muscular arms, and that damn smug grin had me swallowing hard. The heat rushing through me had nothing to do with the water.

I quickly looked away, but I could feel my pulse racing.

Damn it, Kansas. Get a grip.

"Enjoying the view?" Dawson teased.

I rolled my eyes, pretending I hadn't noticed. "You wish," I lied because I most certainly *was* enjoying every inch of him!

Dinner was a feast fit for royalty—lobster, venison, freshly baked bread, and every decadent dish imaginable. I ate like I hadn't seen food in days, completely ignoring the amused looks Dawson threw my way. After all, he probably lived off feasts like this regularly.

Once the plates were cleared, Dawson stood up, extending his hand toward me. "I've got one more surprise for you tonight."

I hesitated for a second before taking it, curiosity getting the better of me. He led me outside into the frigid air, my breath forming small clouds in front of me. We walked toward what I initially thought were cabins, but as we got closer, I realized they were made entirely of glass.

"Glass huts?" I blinked in disbelief, looking around us. "Out here? Are you serious?"

Dawson's lips quirked into a grin. "You better believe it. You haven't experienced anything until you've seen this."

I was in awe. The glass structures shimmered under the moonlight like they belonged in a fantasy world. The vast, snowy landscape, framed by the transparent walls, stretched out around us. I could already imagine lying in one, watching the stars above.

"I'm not sleeping with you," I blurted out as we stepped inside one of the huts, the warmth of the space enveloping me immediately.

Dawson raised an eyebrow, leaning against the wall casually. "I beg to differ."

My jaw dropped, and I was about to fire off a snarky retort when he smirked. "I meant *sleep*, Kansas. Just sleep. But if you want to read into it, I certainly don't mind."

I glared at him, hating how easily he got under my skin. But I was also very aware of how my pulse quickened every time he did.

He opened a bottle of champagne and poured two glasses, handing one to me. I stared at it and remembered my vow to stay away from alcohol. But one glass wouldn't hurt, would it? We clinked glasses, and I couldn't help but get lost in the ambiance. The glass walls framed the sky perfectly, and above us, the Northern Lights began to dance. Swirls of green, blue, and violet painted the heavens, so mesmerizing it took my breath away.

"This is simply... " I trailed off, not finding the words.

"Beautiful," Dawson finished for me, his voice low and soft.

I nodded, taking a sip of the champagne. The bubbles tickled my tongue, and the warmth from the heater wrapped around me like a blanket. I was beginning to feel comfortable—too comfortable.

Don't get caught up in the romance of it all!

When I glanced at Dawson, he watched me, his eyes smoldering under the dim light.

Before I knew what was happening, he stepped closer, his gaze never leaving mine. "Why do you always fight this?" he asked, his voice barely above a whisper.

"I'm not fighting—" I started to say, but my breath hitched as he leaned in.

His lips touched mine, soft at first, but as soon as I kissed him back, the kiss deepened, fiery and consuming. My mind screamed at me to stop, but my body had other ideas. His hands slid to my waist, pulling me closer, and I couldn't think straight anymore.

The Northern Lights swirled overhead, and the champagne was forgotten as we stumbled toward the bed. Our kisses frantic and needy—every touch and look was too much, yet not enough.

"Kansas," Dawson whispered against my throat as he feathered kisses down my neck. His hot breath ignited everything inside me until I couldn't resist.

His hands stripped me of all the layers I was wearing until I stood only in my panties and bra. He continued his kisses down between my breasts, never taking his eyes off me, and I nearly thought I was going to go crazy with need. I raked my hands through his hair and breathed his name.

"Dawson."

I felt him smile against my skin as he made his way down to my center, fingering the silky fabric aside. I groaned, throwing my head back while he tasted what I had to offer. When he finally returned to my lips, I was clawing at him.

We lay naked. "I want you underneath me so you can look up at the Northern Lights while I take you to heaven and back again."

He laced his fingers with mine and drew them over my head while he spread my legs and hovered, looking intensely at me as if asking if this was alright.

Alright? More than alright. But I couldn't find the words, so I simply nodded and bit my lip, which must have sent him over the edge because in half a second, he was deep inside, and I writhed in ecstasy underneath him, watching the Northern Lights. I truly was on the brink of heaven.

We found our rhythm quickly, and as Dawson found his release, he smashed his lips down on mine, biting until he drew blood.

"Ouch!" I said, but a smile tugged at my lip. "You naughty boy!"

He lifted me and maneuvered us so I was on top. "It's my turn to see the lights while you finish yourself off."

His hands snaked around my breasts as I arched my back and took him with my heat, drawing every inch of passion out of him. When I rode my own wave, I looked up at the multi-colored sky and groaned in delight.

Afterward, we lay, satiated and breathless, and somewhere in the back of my mind, I knew this was a bad idea, but at that moment, with Dawson's curled around me, breathing heavily, I never wanted to leave our icy little haven.

Chapter 10:

Dawson

I woke up to the warmth of someone beside me. For a second, I thought I'd dreamed it—being that close to Kansas Stonehouse. But when I opened my eyes, there she was. Her wild hair spread out across the pillow like a golden halo, her soft breathing in sync with the rhythm of the morning. A strange sense of peace washed over me.

Then, reality hit.

Kansas stirred, blinking awake. Her eyes widened the second she realized where she was.

"Oh my God!" she bolted upright, scrambling away from me as if I'd turned into some kind of monster. "Dawson?" Her voice was sharp.

I sat up slowly, keeping my hands raised in defense. "Kansas, wait—"

She cut me off, her face flushed with anger. "I can't believe you! You—rich people are all the same, aren't you? This—this whole glass hut thing was a setup, wasn't it? You thought we'd watch the Northern Lights, get cozy, and then..."

"Stop." My voice was firm, but I kept it low. "That wasn't my intention. At *all*."

She folded her arms across her chest, glaring at me. "Right. So you just happened to book only one glass hut and expected us to share? You just happened to—"

"There was only one glass hut available," I said quickly. "These huts are new. The project just finished. I was supposed to stay in one to make sure it was up to standard. I thought you'd want to see it too. You love nature, the stars, and all of that." I ran a hand through my hair, trying to explain before she got even more worked up. "I was going to put us in separate huts, but they booked up fast, and when I realized how remote this place was, I didn't want anything to happen to you. If something went wrong, I needed to be close by."

Kansas narrowed her eyes, clearly suspicious. "So you figured we'd just enjoy the lights and return to our rooms, huh? And somehow that turned into this?"

"I wasn't planning on spending the night together," I replied, holding her gaze. She clearly missed the part about me wanting to ensure her safety. "We watched the Northern Lights. Then it got late, and we fell asleep. That's all that happened."

She shifted, not quite sure what to believe. "You expect me to just take your word for it?"

"I know you don't trust me, Kansas. I get it. But I'm not trying to manipulate you, and this wasn't some ploy to, you know."

For a moment, there was silence. She looked away, chewing on her bottom lip, the wheels turning in her mind. I could see the battle between her instincts and the walls she'd built. She'd been so guarded from the moment we met. That chip on her shoulder was still sharp.

She stood abruptly, pulling the blanket tighter around her. "I want to leave now."

I nodded, resisting the urge to say more. Pushing her wouldn't help right now. "Of course."

***

Two hours later, we walked up to my private jet, which hummed softly as we made our way to Tuscany, the rolling clouds outside a constant, peaceful backdrop. Kansas sat across from me, her notepad in her lap, pen twirling between her fingers as she studied me with her ever-present frown. Seven and a half hours on a plane with her asking questions felt like an eternity, but we had work to do.

Luckily, she was the kind of person who put our differences aside to get the work done. I appreciated that. I wouldn't have wanted to hash it all out on the trip, but I did want to talk to her about it once we were settled in Tuscany.

"So," she began, breaking the silence. "How old were you when you took over Lancaster Luxury Estates?"

I glanced out the window, collecting my thoughts before answering. "Twenty-eight."

She scribbled down a note. "That's young to run a massive hotel chain. Why so early?"

I kept my face neutral, trying not to let my irritation show. "My father passed unexpectedly from a heart attack. Someone had to step up."

Kansas's eyes flickered to me, a spark of curiosity there. "And your brothers? They didn't want the responsibility?"

"No. They have their own lives."

She made another note. "What about your mother? What was her reaction to your brothers wanting nothing to do with the company?"

I tensed at the mention of my mother. I didn't want to dive into Lorraine's relentless matchmaking attempts right now. "She wasn't thrilled, but she understood the situation."

Kansas pursed her lips, clearly unsatisfied with my answer, but moved on anyway. "What's been the hardest part of running the company?"

I leaned back in my seat, my gaze shifting from her to the clouds. "Managing expectations—of investors, clients, staff. Everyone always wants more."

Kansas tilted her head slightly, her pen hovering over the paper. "And personally? What's been the hardest part for you?"

I hesitated. That question cut a little too deep. "Next question."

She raised an eyebrow but didn't push. "Fine. What's your biggest regret?"

I clenched my jaw slightly. "I'm not answering that."

She sighed, clearly frustrated with my evasiveness. "You realize if I'm going to write your biography, I need more than just surface-level details, right? People want to know who you are, not just the public persona."

I met her gaze, my voice calm but firm. "There are some things I'm not ready to talk about. And you're going to have to accept that."

She scoffed, scribbling something down aggressively. "Of course. The billionaire with walls around his heart. How *original*."

I couldn't help but smirk. "You sound like you're writing the script for a soap opera."

Her eyes flickered with amusement for a brief second before the frown returned. "Maybe I am. You're giving me enough drama."

We spent the next few hours in silence, interrupted only by her occasional questions—some of which I answered, others I refused.

When we landed in Tuscany, the sun was already beginning to set. My hotel loomed in the distance, a modern castle perched on a hill, blending old-world charm with sleek luxury. Kansas glanced at it with awe and skepticism.

"*This* is your hotel?" she asked, her voice laced with disbelief.

I smiled. "Welcome to Lancaster Tuscany. Let's see if it lives up to your standards."

She didn't reply, but I caught the brief flicker of admiration in her eyes. Maybe I was starting to break through that giant chip on her shoulder.

***

The Tuscan sunset bathed the vineyard in subdued light as we walked along the rows of vines. The air was rich with the scent of grapes, lavender, and earth—a perfect evening, or so I thought. Kansas was uncharacteristically quiet, her usual sharp retorts replaced by a calmness I rarely saw in her.

"This place is beautiful," she said softly, almost reluctantly.

I glanced at her, a small smile tugging at my lips. "Glad you think so. It's one of my favorite properties."

She scoffed lightly, but there was no bite to it. "Of course, you'd own a vineyard in Tuscany." She rolled her eyes, which I didn't appreciate.

We reached a clearing where a small dinner table had been set up. The view was breathtaking—miles of vineyards stretching out beneath the setting sun. The table was adorned with wine glasses and plates of fresh Italian cuisine.

"I figured you'd appreciate the atmosphere," I said, pulling out a chair for her.

Kansas sat, eying the food and the setup with suspicion and awe. "What's the catch?"

I chuckled. "No catch. Just dinner."

We ate in relative silence, the usual tension between us softened by the beauty of the surroundings. For a moment, it felt like we weren't bickering business partners but two people simply enjoying each other's company.

After dinner, I led her to the surprise I'd planned—a hot-air balloon ride over the vineyard. Her eyes widened as she saw the balloon's colorful fabric stretching out into the sky.

"Are you serious?" she asked, her voice betraying a hint of excitement mixed with nerves.

"It's Tuscany. You can't say no to a hot-air balloon ride here."

She hesitated but eventually nodded, following me into the basket. As the balloon lifted, I could see her grip on the edge tightening.

"You alright?" I asked, noticing the way her knuckles had turned white.

"I'm fine," she muttered, but her voice wavered.

We rose higher, the vineyard becoming a patchwork of greens and purples beneath us. But Kansas wasn't looking at the view anymore. Her face had paled, and sweat was beading on her forehead.

"Kansas, are you okay?"

She didn't answer. Her eyes fluttered shut, and before I could reach out, she collapsed.

Panic surged through me. I quickly signaled the operator to bring us down. When we landed, I carried her back to the car, racing to the hotel which was just down the road.

By the time she woke up, we were back in my suite, and she was lying in my bed. Her eyes blinked open, confusion crossing her face before she groaned.

"Dawson?"

"I'm here," I said, sitting on the edge of the bed. "Why didn't you say you weren't feeling well?"

She winced, sitting up slowly. "I didn't think it would bother me."

I frowned. "I had my doctor on call check you out, and he says you'll be just fine. The traveling might have gotten to you."

Kansas glared at me, her usual fire returning. "You had a doctor check me out? I'm not fragile, but I *am* afraid of heights."

"Yes, I did, and I didn't say you were," I replied, keeping my tone calm. I shook my head. "But you scared the hell out of me back there."

She scowled, pulling the covers around her. "I'm fine. I don't need a babysitter."

I chuckled, knowing she was a bad patient, but I wasn't going anywhere. "Too bad. You've got one anyway."

I settled onto the couch next to Kansas, her exhaustion evident in the way she leaned into me. I wrapped my arm around her, pulling her closer, careful not to push any boundaries. We watched a movie in comfortable silence, her head resting on my chest, the rhythmic rise and fall of her breathing grounding me.

"You're staying?" she murmured, eyes half-closed.

"Yes. I'm not leaving." My voice was softer than I intended.

She nodded, pressing into me again. We didn't need to say more. Tonight was about comfort, nothing else—just the two of us, in this moment, together.

Chapter 11:

Kansas

I woke up to the sound of Dawson's soft breathing beside me, his arm draped over my waist. I couldn't believe he stayed all night. My heart swelled; it wasn't something I hadn't expected from him. I carefully slipped out of bed, not wanting to wake him. Dawson Lancaster, the man I was supposed to hate, had a way of chipping away at my defenses, one quiet moment at a time.

After getting dressed, I headed toward the living room, ready to explore the castle. I reached for the door handle, but a sharp knock interrupted my thoughts. I opened the door to a tall, stunning blonde with striking amber eyes.

"Can I help you?" I asked, eying her cautiously. I figured she must be one of Dawson's employees.

Her smile faded as she looked me over from head to toe, her gaze lingering on my clothes. "I'm an old friend of Dawson's. Lara Robertson," she said, her voice calm and measured.

I crossed my arms. "Dawson's still sleeping."

A flicker of something—jealousy, maybe—crossed her face, and her jaw tightened. "That's fine. I'll wait inside. He'll want to see me."

Her confidence threw me off. I hesitated, unsure of how to respond. I'd planned to leave, but the thought of her sitting here, waiting for Dawson, made my stomach twist.

"I was just about to head out," I said slowly.

Lara's eyes sparkled with something I couldn't read. "That's okay. You can leave. What I need to talk to Dawson about is very private."

Private? My instincts told me to stay, but I found myself nodding. "Right. I'll see you later."

I couldn't shake the unease gnawing at me as I walked out. Lara's presence felt like a storm on the horizon, and I spent the rest of the day wondering if I'd made a huge mistake leaving her alone with Dawson.

As I wandered through the halls of the Lancaster Luxury Estates, I couldn't shake the thought of Lara and Dawson back in his room. Every step felt heavier, my mind conjuring images of them talking, laughing, or worse. Why did I leave him with nothing but his boxers on? I took my time admiring the castle's grand architecture, the stunning chandeliers, the polished marble floors, and the sweeping ocean views, but none of it could distract me for long.

The thought of that bombshell with him had my stomach in knots.

Hours passed. I couldn't take it anymore. I found myself back at his door, knocking lightly at first, then harder. No answer.

Fine. I went to my own room, pacing the floor, hoping he'd call. But after another hour, still nothing. The unease was building—no, it was jealousy— a feeling I hated because I wasn't supposed to care. I was *not* supposed to like Dawson Lancaster, the arrogant, ultra-rich control freak. Yet here I was, feeling like an idiot for leaving him alone with her.

I decided to go swimming, hoping to cool my nerves. The water felt good, but it did nothing for the tightness in my chest. After a long swim, I showered, hoping he'd text or call. But there was still nothing by the time two more hours rolled by.

Frustrated, I texted him. Then I called. Still no response.

I went to dinner alone, trying to push the thoughts of him—and Lara—out of my head. It didn't work.

After dinner, I called Shellene.

"You need to stop worrying," she said, her voice full of that carefree vibe only she could pull off. "Go to the bar; find a nice man to keep you company. When Dawson shows up, *he'll* be the jealous one."

"Shellene, I don't even—" I started, but she cut me off.

"Don't even what? Like him? Please, Kansas, I know you. You're jealous because you care. So go make him squirm for once."

I sighed, unsure if I had it in me to follow her advice. But the idea of making Dawson jealous was very tempting, so I headed to the bar.

The bar was dimly lit, conversation and the clink of glasses filling the air. I slid onto a stool, trying to shake off the irritation gnawing at me. My eyes caught on a man sitting a few seats down—a nice-looking guy with dark hair and a warm smile.

"Mind if I sit here?" I asked, nodding toward the stool next to him.

"Not at all," he said, flashing a grin. "I'm Jared." What a great smile! His teeth were perfectly straight and white.

"Kansas," I replied, and we quickly slipped into easy conversation. Jared was funny and charming, and I laughed more than I had all day. I felt a little lighter for the first time since leaving Dawson's room.

But then, out of the corner of my eye, I saw Dawson striding into the bar with that familiar air of authority, his expression unreadable—until his gaze landed on me.

I knew what I had to do.

Leaning a little closer to Jared, I placed my hand on his, feeling the warmth of his skin under mine. "So, tell me more about your trip," I said, making my voice as sweet as I could muster. Jared didn't seem to notice the shift in my focus, his face lighting up as he continued to talk.

But I wasn't listening. I was watching Dawson.

His expression darkened, the easygoing charm he usually wore wiped away, replaced by something colder. His eyes flicked to my hand on Jared's, and I could see the tension in his jaw. *Good.* Let him stew.

I laughed at something Jared said, though I hadn't really heard it, making a point to ignore Dawson's approach. My pulse quickened, not from Jared's company but from the knowledge that Dawson was watching, and for the first time, I had the upper hand.

"Enjoying yourself?" Dawson's deep voice finally cut through the air, cold as ice.

I barely glanced his way. "Oh, I didn't see you there," I said casually, though the quick thrum of my heart betrayed me.

Dawson's eyes narrowed. I could see the storm brewing, and for some reason, it felt thrilling.

"Meet me in my room. Now!" Dawson said, his voice a low command that sent a shiver down my spine. He didn't wait for an answer before turning on his heel and walking out of the bar.

I let out a breath, trying to compose myself. Jared, the guy at the bar, raised an eyebrow. "So, is he your boyfriend?"

I shook my head, forcing a smile. "No, he's not."

Jared chuckled softly. "Could've fooled me. He sure looked like a man in love."

That comment hit harder than I expected. Love? Dawson Lancaster? The thought was ridiculous, wasn't it?

"Excuse me," I muttered, grabbing my purse and heading for Dawson's room. I wasn't ready for whatever this would be, but I wasn't about to back down, either.

When I got to his door, I knocked sharply. He opened it almost immediately, stepping aside for me to enter. The tension in the air was thick enough to choke on.

"What the hell was that all about?" I snapped, folding my arms.

He closed the door, his expression hard. Dawson ignored my question and asked, "What were you doing with that guy at the bar?"

I laughed, but there was no humor in it. I decided to ignore his question. "Really? That's what you want to talk about? I'm not here to twiddle my thumbs, Dawson. I'm here to work on your book, which, by the way, is going nowhere because you've been MIA all day. Who is Lara?"

His jaw tightened. "She's my ex-girlfriend."

The words stung more than they should have. "So, you spent the entire day catching up with your ex, and it didn't even occur to you to send me a message to let me know I was on my own?"

"I didn't think you needed your hand held," he shot back, his voice cold. "And it's none of your business where I was."

My stomach twisted. "It is when I'm stuck here wondering where you are. I was under the impression we would be working on your book."

Dawson crossed his arms, his eyes narrowing. "You seemed fine chatting up some random guy at the bar. Who is he?"

"He's a nice man. I enjoyed his company, and that's *all*," I said, letting the words sting as I knew they would.

His eyes darkened. "I'm not paying you to pick up men, Kansas."

"That's rich coming from the guy who disappeared with his ex!" I snapped.

We stood there, glaring at each other, unwilling to back down. The silence between us was a storm, ready to break.

He finally shrugged and said, "I think we should stop discussing this and work, as you said."

I said nothing and sat down.

The heat between Dawson and me grew as we attempted to work. His voice sent a shiver down my spine every time he spoke, and I hated it. I hate that I cared. The truth hit me like a freight train—I was jealous—jealous of Lara, their past, and whatever they were doing all day.

I shouldn't be. It was a fling, a mistake I wouldn't make again. I decided right then and there, no more. I wouldn't let myself fall for him, not when I disliked everything he stood for.

But as we worked, my resolve wavered. He was infuriatingly sexy, his presence impossible to ignore. The way he leaned over the desk, the flex of his muscles beneath his shirt—I could hardly concentrate. By the time we wrapped up, I was desperate to get away, to clear my head.

I stood, ready to bolt. "I'll be going now. Sleep well."

But before I could escape, Dawson grabbed my arm, turning me to face him. In one swift move, he backed me against the wall and kissed me hard. I squirmed, trying to get away, but my body betrayed me, melting into his touch. His hands slid under my blouse, sending heat through my veins.

Then, an image of Lara flashed into my mind, and I shoved him back, breathless. "I'm *leaving*," I repeated, my voice shaking.

He didn't follow.

Back in my hotel room, I headed straight for the shower, hoping the hot water would wash away the turmoil inside me. But as soon as the water hit my skin, the tears came.

I pressed my forehead against the cool tile, sobbing quietly, overwhelmed by the intensity of my feelings for Dawson. How had I let this happen? He was everything I claimed to despise—wealthy, controlling, unreachable.

But my heart didn't care. The way he made me feel was terrifying. How much longer could I ignore it?

I sank to the floor, whispering, "I can't do this."

Chapter 12:

Dawson

I sat at the head of the polished mahogany conference table, waiting for my managers, Shawna and Derek, and executives to arrive. Kansas sat beside me, scribbling notes in her leather-bound journal. I caught her eye for a moment, but she quickly looked away. She still hadn't warmed up to me, though I'd be lying if I said her disdain wasn't intriguing.

Shawna and Derek walked in, both looking sharp and professional as always. Shawna, head of customer relations, was all about efficiency, while Derek, who ran our operations, thrived on precision. Both were key players in Lancaster Luxury Estates' success. Eight other executives filed in and took their seats, each smiling, nodding at me, and taking a sideways glance at Kansas.

I cleared my throat and gestured toward Kansas. "Before we start, I'd like to introduce Kansas Stonehouse. She's an advisor for a special project I'm working on. She'll be sitting in on today's meeting."

Shawna and Derek exchanged glances, but neither questioned me. One of the perks of leadership—I didn't owe anyone an explanation, but I habitually gave them anyway. I knew how to balance authority with fairness.

"We're here to talk about a few things," I continued, "but primarily, I want us to focus on the feedback from guests regarding the online check-in system. I've been hearing mixed reviews, and I think we can do better."

Shawna nodded. "We've had complaints about the app being too complicated. Some guests say they prefer the traditional check-in experience."

"And that's where we're losing efficiency," Derek added, leaning forward. "I've run the numbers. Manual check-ins increase wait times by an average of twelve minutes per guest. We can't afford that if we're pushing a luxury experience."

Kansas looked up from her notes. "What about making the online process more personal?" Her voice was calm but firm. "Maybe there's a way to blend the convenience of online check-in with the personalized touch that keeps people coming back."

Derek glanced at me, waiting for my reaction. I nodded, encouraging the conversation. "Go on, Kansas."

"Well, think about it. What if we allowed guests to upload a voice or video message during check-in? Something where they can say what they're most excited about or what their preferences are. It could make the process feel less transactional."

Shawna's eyes lit up. "That could work. And we could send them a welcome video from the hotel manager or even you, Dawson. It adds a layer of personalization without sacrificing speed."

"I like it," I said. "We need to make the guests feel valued from the moment they check in. Anything else we can tweak?"

Derek grinned. "We could also offer them customizable room features they can choose during check-in. Mood lighting, music preferences, and even pillow types. Make them feel like they're shaping their stay."

I smiled. This was why I trusted my team—they didn't just follow orders; they contributed. "I want prototypes for these ideas within a week. Let's make it happen."

As they left, I could see the renewed energy in their step. Shawna turned back with a smile. "Good call bringing Kansas in. She's sharp."

I glanced at Kansas, but she was already lost in her notes again.

After the managers and executives left, Kansas turned to me, her eyes bright with admiration she probably didn't realize she was showing.

"That was amazing to watch," she said, her voice full of awe, though I doubted she'd admit it if I pressed.

I couldn't resist teasing her. "Are you saying you're in awe of me, Kansas? That's a first."

She shot me a look that could freeze water. "In awe of you? Hardly. I love how you interact with your staff. They obviously highly respect you, yet you're not authoritative with them. It's refreshing to see."

I chuckled. "I'll take that as a compliment."

A few hours later, the moment lingered as we headed toward the airport. I could tell she wasn't used to being impressed by someone like me. I filed it away, knowing I'd probably needle her about it later.

Once we boarded my plane to Vermont, I glanced over at her. "By the way, my parents live there. Don't say I didn't warn you."

She raised an eyebrow. "Warn me? What, do they eat poor writers for dinner?"

"Not usually," I said with a smirk, "but they might make an exception."

The flight was long, and we barely spoke. Kansas was absorbed in her book and then worked on a crossword puzzle before finally drifting off to sleep. I couldn't take my eyes off her—each little habit of hers fascinated me. The way she brushed her hair behind her ear when reading or the quiet determination on her face when solving a puzzle. She looked peaceful when she slept, contrasting her usual sharp wit and sarcastic remarks.

Desire stirred in me, something I wasn't expecting. I found myself wondering what she was thinking when she was quiet and how she'd react if she knew the effect she had on me. But I kept that to myself—for now.

***

We sat across from each other in my office at the Vermont Lancaster location, papers spread out on the polished cherry wood table. The room felt too small, even though it was massive—probably because Kansas's presence was electric.

"So, the chapter about your first hotel," Kansas said, her voice even but her fingers gripping her pen tightly, "I think we should dig deeper into the personal challenges you faced. Readers will connect more if you're honest."

I leaned back in my chair, folding my arms. "I don't know if I need to bare my soul, Kansas. This is a biography, not a therapy session."

Her eyes flashed with frustration, and I could tell she was holding back. "Well, if you want people to care about you, maybe showing you're more than just a *rich* guy with an empire wouldn't hurt."

My jaw tightened. She always knew exactly where to strike. "I didn't get here by being soft."

"No one's asking you to be soft," she snapped, then took a breath, her chest rising. "But maybe if you showed a little vulnerability, it'd help your image."

"There is nothing wrong with my image," I sighed, looking down at the notes she'd scribbled. We'd been at this for hours, and despite the constant friction, we were getting a lot done. But the way she kept pushing me—testing me—was driving me insane.

Still, I couldn't deny how much I admired her fire. "Fine," I said, my voice lower, calmer. "We'll add more detail. But don't expect a sob story."

Kansas met my gaze, her lips twitching into a smirk. "Wouldn't dream of it."

The sparks between us were undeniable, but I forced myself to focus on the work. If I let myself slip, I knew I'd want her—more than just professionally.

***

We arrived in Burlington just before dawn, exhausted from the long flight. The hotel lobby was quiet, bathed in early morning light as we checked in. Kansas looked exhausted, dark circles under her eyes betraying her fatigue. We checked into the hotel—another one of mine, naturally—and headed to our separate rooms without a word, each desperate for sleep and a hot shower. I needed time to clear my head before tonight.

I collapsed onto the bed, intending to rest for a few hours. When I woke to my alarm, the clock read 3:00 p.m. After a quick shower, I dressed and headed to Kansas's suite. Knocking firmly, I waited. The door opened a crack, and she peered out, her hair damp from a recent shower.

She raised an eyebrow. "What do you want?"

"Be ready in one hour," I said, leaning casually against the door frame.

She folded her arms, clearly not in the mood for games. "Ready for what?"

"We're going to my parent's for dinner," I informed her.

Her eyes widened, and I caught the brief flicker of unease before she masked it with her usual sarcasm. "Your parents? You never mentioned we were going there tonight."

"I just did," I replied with a faint smile. She had no idea what she was in for. "One hour."

She sighed. "Fine. But a little warning next time would be nice."

"Consider this your warning," I said.

"How very nice of you to spring this on me last minute." She rolled her eyes.

I rubbed the back of my neck, not thrilled about the situation myself. "It wasn't part of the plan," I admitted. "But my father wants to talk about the hotel business, and I don't have much choice. It's easier to go along with it."

She crossed her arms, clearly not impressed. "I'm going to feel really out of place while you have your family meeting."

I shook my head, trying to soften the blow. "My brothers, Preston and Hutton, flew in yesterday. They'll be there too. It's more of a dinner with the family. You'll be fine."

Her eyebrows shot up. "I'm meeting your parents *and* your brothers?" She let out a small, frustrated laugh.

"Don't sound so panicked. I'm not thrilled about it either, Kansas," I said, keeping my tone calm. "I'm not exactly close with them, especially my father. But it's unavoidable, and we must play nice for the night."

She paused, looking at me with a mixture of disbelief and curiosity. "Why do I get the feeling you're dreading this more than I am?"

"Because I am," I said with a dry smile. "Just don't mention the book. They don't know I've hired someone to write my biography. Let's keep that part quiet."

She nodded slowly, still processing. "Fine. But you owe me for this."

As I walked back to my room, I couldn't shake the feeling that dinner tonight would be more intense than any boardroom negotiation. Kansas might not know it yet, but this wasn't just any family dinner.

Chapter 13:

Kansas

Dawson was unusually quiet as we drove to his parents. I glanced at him, his hands gripping the steering wheel a little too tightly. Even when he was upset, he was incredibly sexy. I hated this—being in the dark, unsure of what was going on with him. Finally, I couldn't take it anymore.

"Is something wrong?" I asked, keeping my voice light though my insides were churning.

He hesitated, his eyes fixed on the road. "I'm not exactly *close* with my parents." His words were clipped like he was holding back something bigger. "But you'll get a lot of material for the book during this visit."

My stomach dropped. "What do you mean?"

Dawson didn't answer; he just kept driving and left my question hanging in the air like a bad omen. I suddenly became nervous about what awaited me at his parents' house. If his family were anything like him, this would be a long, awkward visit.

When we finally pulled up, I blinked in surprise. This wasn't the luxurious mansion I was expecting. Instead, it was one of the smallest houses in an old neighborhood, weathered and desperately needing repair. The paint peeled off the siding, and the yard was overgrown with weeds. My mouth went dry. This was nothing like the lavishness I'd come to expect from Dawson Lancaster.

I froze, staring at the house, and then turned to Dawson. His expression was unreadable, but his gaze was sharp.

"Not what you expected, is it?" His eyebrow quirked up, and I could hear the challenge in his voice.

I swallowed, unsure of how to respond. "No," I admitted.

"Everything you learn over the next few days," he said, his tone softening, "will make you understand. This part of my story needs to be told—not the excessively wealthy part."

I stared at him, unable to form words. What had I just walked into?

My heart thudded as we approached the front door, and I realized I was holding my breath. I glanced at Dawson, whose jaw was tight, his usual confidence replaced by something more guarded. Before I could ask, the door swung open, revealing a man dressed in a police uniform. He was tall and dark like Dawson and did look like a brother, but he was nowhere near as handsome.

"Hey, Dawson. Kansas, right? I'm Dawson's middle brother, Preston. Come on in," he said with a warm smile, stepping aside.

We walked into the modest living room, a far cry from the luxury I'd associated with Dawson. Another dark-haired man was lounging on the couch watching TV. He was definitely Dawson's brother, but much younger. Another man sat in a worn recliner. He was much older—I assumed he was their father.

The man looked up briefly, his expression stern. "Well, if it isn't the big man on campus. Come home to see his parents for what, the second time this year?"

I froze, shocked by the bitterness in his tone. Dawson remained composed, but his voice held a trace of sadness as he replied, "Nice to see you too, Father. Kansas, this is my father, Frederick."

My stomach twisted as I saw the flicker of pain in Dawson's eyes.

When Dawson introduced me, Frederick didn't even glance at me, but the younger man stood up and extended his hand. "I'm the youngest, Hutton, and obviously the best looking." He smirked, but somehow I didn't think he was joking. I think he actually thought it was true.

As we stepped into the kitchen, the scent of something simmering filled the air. Dawson's mother, Rebecca, stood at the stove, stirring a pot. Her back was straight, and her movements were efficient. She glanced over her shoulder as we entered, her eyes landing on Dawson first.

"Dawson," she said coolly, without the warmth you'd expect from a mother greeting her son. Her gaze then flicked to Preston and Hutton, a softer smile gracing her lips. "Preston, Hutton, good to see you both."

"Hey, Mom," Hutton said, pulling her into a light hug. Preston merely smiled and winked at her.

Dawson, on the other hand, just nodded. "Mom."

Rebecca barely acknowledged him, giving him only a quick, dismissive glance before returning to the stove. "Dinner will be ready soon."

Wow. I couldn't believe how different she acted with them. It was as if Dawson was merely a guest in his own family, not her son.

I stood there awkwardly, watching the interactions unfold. How could she be so cold to him? Always so confident and in control, Dawson seemed to shrink slightly in his mother's presence, and I could surely see why that was.

He turned to me, his expression unreadable, and I could see the layers of tension beneath his calm demeanor. "Kansas, this is my mother, Rebecca."

"Nice to meet you," I said, offering a smile.

Rebecca glanced at me briefly, nodding. "Everyone, have a seat and help yourself." She practically ignored me. I was shocked by the inhospitality.

Dinner was a strange mix of noise and tension. His mother and brothers carried the conversation, their voices dominating the table. Dawson, on the other hand, barely spoke. When he did, it was only to be met with his mother's condescending responses.

"So, Dawson, how's the female search?" Rebecca asked, her tone thick with sarcasm. "Still working far too hard to have fun?"

Dawson's jaw clenched. "I'm not searching for females, and you know that."

She scoffed and turned back to Preston and Hutton, who were busy bragging about their own lives. "Preston's dating a new woman who works as a detective from his precinct," Rebecca said, her pride evident. "And Hutton, I hear you're considering asking Maggie to marry you. Honestly, you boys make me proud."

I could hardly believe the arrogance dripping from every word. The way they talked about themselves was nauseating, as if the world revolved around them.

Dawson stayed quiet. Meanwhile, his father, Frederick, knocked back another drink, barely participating in the conversation beyond an occasional grunt. I counted six drinks with dinner.

No one asked me anything. They didn't even seem to notice I was there. It was beyond rude, and I felt invisible, sitting at this crumbling dinner table in a house that looked like it might fall apart any minute. Why hadn't Dawson helped them out financially? The house was in shambles. Maybe that was the source of all this tension—Dawson refused to give them money.

The thought unsettled me. I glanced at him, wondering if that was the truth behind the cold distance between him and his family.

About an hour later, when Dawson stepped out to pull the car around, I felt a presence behind me. I turned and saw Rebecca, her eyes cold as they fixed on me.

"You should look elsewhere for a suitable mate," she said, her voice like ice. "My son is not for someone like you. We both know why you're really here—his *money*. But let me make something clear: Dawson already has the love of his life, Lara. You'd do well to stay out of her way."

Her words hit me like a punch. I whirled around to face her, anger rising in my chest. "Money? Is that what you think?"

Rebecca narrowed her eyes. "I think you and I both know that's what you're after."

I had to contain my anger. "Maybe you should get to know your son better. If you did, you'd know there's much more to him than his bank account!"

Her eyebrows raised like she was going to reply, but I wasn't going to stand there and listen to her poison.

I turned and stormed out. My heart pounded as I walked away, refusing to look back. I kept my mouth shut when I saw Dawson waiting by the car, smiling like nothing had happened. This was between me and his mother— and she was wrong about me.

Dead wrong.

As soon as we got in the car, an uneasy silence settled between us. My mind kept circling back to what Rebecca had said. I stared out the window, but the question burned on my tongue until I couldn't hold it in any longer.

"Why haven't you helped your parents financially?" I asked, keeping my tone steady but direct.

Dawson's hands tightened on the steering wheel, his jaw clenching. "Are you really going to accuse me of not helping my parents?" he shot back, his voice laced with irritation. "Don't you think I've tried? Their pride won't let them accept it. I've offered, but they refuse every time."

His words hung in the air, sharp and biting. I hadn't expected that response, and guilt tugged at me for assuming the worst. "I didn't mean to accuse you," I said, my voice softer now. "I don't understand why they'd turn down help when it's right there."

"It's like they don't want to acknowledge that I made Dad's business far more successful than he ever could," he muttered, eyes fixed ahead. "They'd rather struggle than accept my money. It's a pride thing."

Silence stretched between us again, heavy and awkward. When we arrived back at the hotel, Dawson parked the car and turned to me, his expression unreadable. "I'm going to retire to my room for the night," he said, his voice detached. "I'll see you tomorrow."

I blinked, stunned. "Oh, okay," I managed, feeling confused and off-balance as he walked away.

Alone in my room later, I couldn't settle. My mind replayed the conversation, the tension lingering long after Dawson had disappeared. Nothing about this made sense, and I had no idea how to feel.

Chapter 14:

Dawson

I had reached my limit.

"We're going home tomorrow," I told Kansas abruptly as we stood in my parent's small backyard overlooking the small flower garden my mother had planted years before but never weeded. My father's presence still loomed, even when he wasn't there. I could see the question forming on her lips, but she didn't ask. Her silence spoke volumes, and I didn't have the patience to elaborate.

She simply nodded. "Okay."

The following day, we were on the plane, the sound of the engines doing little to drown out the heaviness that lingered in the air. Kansas finally broke the silence.

"Do you want to work on the book?" she asked, her voice softer than usual, as if she could sense the unease I was trying so hard to bury.

I shook my head. "Not in the mood."

That was all I said, and she didn't press me. Instead, she pulled out her notebook and got to work, scribbling away like it was the only thing in the world that mattered. I watched her, completely absorbed, her focus unwavering.

I couldn't put my finger on why she fascinated me so much, but it was undeniable. The way she poured herself into her work, her thoughts seemed to flow like they had no choice but to come out, and she didn't let anything, not even my moods, sway her. She was her own person: strong, creative, determined. And it hit me then, clear as day—I loved her personality.

I wasn't sure what to do with that.

***

When we got back to my place, something shifted inside me. The tension that had knotted up my chest all morning unraveled a little. As we walked through the front doors, I glanced at Kansas, her face still focused, determined, the same as when we'd been on the plane. Maybe it was the heat of Miami or the simple need for a change of pace, but I found myself suggesting something out of character.

"Why don't we work outside?" I said. Something about being home made me feel better. My place was my sanctuary, and I loved how safe and peaceful it was, blocking out the world's chaos.

Kansas looked surprised but then nodded. "Sure. Sounds nice." I couldn't get over how naturally beautiful she was.

We settled on the patio, the breeze from the ocean brushing past us as I spread out the notes on the table. Loki and Nika lay at our feet, content with the afternoon sun. My usual edge was gone—I could feel it, but it didn't bother me like it should have.

We dove into the work, and to my surprise, we made real progress. She asked questions, her pen scratching away at the paper as I answered. The more I tried to ignore her beauty and push down the strange pull I felt, the more it clawed its way back up to the surface.

I caught myself watching her more than working, mesmerized by how she chewed on the tip of her pen when she was deep in thought, the way her eyes lit up when she hit on an idea.

This wasn't supposed to happen. But the more I fought it, the more I could feel it taking over.

***

Several hours later, I couldn't take it anymore.

Kansas sat across from me, her eyes glued to the laptop screen as she typed furiously. Every now and then, she would tuck a stray strand of hair behind her ear, completely lost in the work. But I wasn't focused on the book anymore. I was focused on her.

The feelings bubbling up inside me were becoming unbearable. I needed space, or at least an excuse to breathe without the distraction of her presence.

"You should take the night off," I said suddenly, the words tumbling out before I could stop them.

Kansas looked up, startled. "What? Why?" She eyed me, and I guess she could see it wasn't a suggestion; it was more like a soft order. "Are you sure?"

I nodded, trying to keep my tone casual. "Yeah. You've earned it. Go spend time with your sisters, friends, or whatever you do when you're not here."

She seemed hesitant for a moment, but then her expression softened. "Alright, thanks. I'll be back tomorrow."

She gathered her things and left, and the house felt strangely empty without her. At first, I welcomed the silence, leaning back in my chair and closing my eyes. But not even ten minutes had passed before a wave of regret crashed over me.

I missed her. *Already.*

It hit me like a punch to the gut. I had practically pushed her out the door, thinking I needed space. Now, all I could think about was how her presence filled the room, her voice, and how she smiled when she was in her element.

I groaned, running a hand through my hair. I had no idea what to do with this feeling, but one thing was clear—I wanted her back.

I needed a distraction, so I called Ritter.

An hour later, we were at his favorite pool hall. The place was dimly lit, with the smell of beer and chalk. Ritter leaned against his cue, watching me line up a shot. I missed, of course—my mind wasn't on the game.

"You're off tonight, man," Ritter said with a smirk, taking his turn. "What's up?"

I sighed, rubbing my temple. "It's Kansas. I gave her the night off, but I don't know now. I can't seem to stop thinking about her."

Ritter chuckled, sinking the ball with ease. "Of course, you can't. You're fighting something that's already a done deal."

I glared at him. "It's not that simple."

"Sure it is." He set up another shot, eyes narrowing. "You're into her, and don't even bother denying it. You've been holding back, probably because you think you can control everything. But you can't control feelings, man."

I stayed quiet, watching the balls scatter across the table. Ritter was right, as much as I hated to admit it.

"You should give in to it," he continued, standing upright and tossing me the cue ball. "Tell her your story. *All of it.* You've been putting it off far too long."

I looked down at the cue ball in my hand. He wasn't wrong. Kansas had been working on my biography, but I'd given her only surface-level details—enough to do the job but not enough to really know me.

Perhaps it was time to change that.

***

I leaned back in the lounge chair by the pool, watching the moonlight dance on the water's surface. I wondered what Kansas had gotten up to, as it was almost midnight. I knew she'd been with her sisters, Mindy and Alyssa, and from what I'd gathered about her relationship with them, those visits could either be relaxing or emotionally exhausting. I supposed she also could be with her friend, Shellene. I glanced at my watch just as I heard the soft click of the gate.

Kansas stepped into view, her figure silhouetted by the soft fairy lights. She paused when she saw me waiting for her, clearly not expecting anyone to be up.

"You're awfully late," I said casually, standing and walking toward her. "Fancy a swim?"

Her hesitation was written all over her face, and I could tell she was mulling over an excuse.

"I don't know, it's pretty late," she replied hesitantly.

I smiled, keeping my tone light. "I won't bite, Kansas. It'll help you unwind. Besides, you're already here, so you might as well keep me company."

She sighed but finally nodded, "I'll go change."

"No need. Whatever you've got on under that pretty dress is probably equivalent to a bikini."

She shrugged and took off the dress. I shouldn't have watched her. I should have closed my eyes and waited for her to get into the pool because the sight before me was awakening every sexual feeling I had. The lacy bra and panties were so inviting, and I really had to control myself as she slipped into the pool. She seemed completely unaware of my body's appreciation of how sexy she was.

I turned and did some laps to work off my sexual tension, swearing I wouldn't kiss her.

A few minutes later, we floated lazily, and I broke the silence. "So, how was your visit? Anything exciting?"

Kansas swirled the water with her hand. "Just the usual. Mindy being practical, and Alyssa is still living in her dream world. And me trying to figure out how to get us all to sell the house."

I nodded. "Do they want to sell the house too?"

She nodded. "Yeah, it's what we need. I just have to make it a reality by earning enough."

"I can tack on an extra $100,000 if that will help," I suggested. Why was I just giving my money away like it was a tissue?

Her eyes widened, and her jaw dropped. "Stop doing that."

"Stop doing what?"

"Throwing money at me like it's nothing. If you had any idea what it was like growing up with my parents… " She broke off, her bottom lip wavering ever so slightly.

I could tell she was holding something back, and I needed to understand her. I asked quietly, "Tell me about your past. What happened with your parents?"

She stiffened, her eyes fixed on the water. "It's not easy to talk about," she muttered.

I waited, giving her space.

She sighed, her voice cracking as she finally spoke. "Our house burned down. My mom left a candle burning, and we lost everything." She swallowed hard, blinking away tears. "The insurance money helped my sisters and I get the small house we're currently in, but it's so cramped. I want out. I want my own space." Her words were sharp as she turned to face me. "But I can't afford it. Not like you. You have this ridiculously extravagant life and take it all for granted."

I felt my temper flare, but I let her continue. "You have no idea what it's like! How awful it is to grow up with next to nothing, barely able to make ends meet! It was so hard losing my parents. I would give anything to have them back. And you! You won't even try to make peace with yours. Do you know how lucky you are that both your parents are still alive?"

That hit deep. Furious, I stood and disappeared inside, gathering my thoughts. When I returned, I handed her a box. "Go to your room and open it."

Her brows furrowed. "What's inside?"

"Go. I don't want to see you again until you've read everything."

She hesitated but left me with the simmering anger I hadn't expected.

Chapter 15:

Kansas

I came downstairs, expecting to find Dawson at his usual spot by the pool, maybe sipping his black coffee while ignoring me like he had a million times before. But this morning, he was nowhere to be found. The empty chairs and the silence felt heavier than usual.

I thought about knocking on his bedroom door but quickly dismissed the idea. He'd made it very clear last night—he didn't want to see me until I'd finished reading. The box of journals sat in my room, full of his life, thoughts, and secrets. I wasn't ready to face all that just yet.

Instead, I made my way to the kitchen. The chef, Nora, greeted me with a polite smile. "Miss Stonehouse, what can I get for you?"

"Scrambled eggs and guacamole, please," I replied, not feeling particularly hungry but knowing I needed something in my stomach. Nora was such a lovely lady, and we chit-chatted while she cooked. I watched her, hoping I would learn something.

Once breakfast was ready, I set myself up on the side patio under the gazebo and beside a beautiful garden. I stared at the journals, all in his handwriting, the first one dating back to when he was a young teenager. I flipped through the pages, my eyes skimming his pen's bold, confident strokes.

How could someone who seemed so sure of everything have such a complicated past?

I sighed, taking a bite of my perfectly cooked eggs. Dawson's life was laid out before me, but for the first time, it didn't feel like I was just writing his biography. It felt like I was about to unravel a part of him he didn't show to anyone—not willingly, at least.

I sat under the gazebo, the heat of the Miami sun softened by the shade around me. Dawson's journals were spread across the table, a tangible weight of a life I hadn't imagined. Each page told a story, not of the billionaire I thought I knew, but of a boy who had clawed his way through hell and back.

The disturbing details of his childhood were written with a rawness that stung. Dawson grew up in a dilapidated neighborhood where kids played on cracked sidewalks and houses leaned too far to one side. But it was the descriptions of his mother that hit me the hardest. She wasn't the poised, cold woman I'd envisioned. She was broken; panic attacks, depression, and anger that boiled over into violence. She had been in and out of mental facilities for most of his life.

I could picture Dawson as a boy, sitting in their small, cramped living room, waiting for her to return, wondering if this time would be any different. He wrote about how he used to hold her when she was at her worst, how she would cry in his arms until she fell asleep, and how, even as a kid, he felt responsible for her.

He was alone. His father was absent in every way that mattered, only showing up to throw fists or shout about how worthless they were. Dawson's brothers didn't help. They ganged up on him, bullying him relentlessly. He described nights spent hiding from them, locking himself in his room, and trying to be invisible. The image of this young boy, beaten down by his own family, made my heart ache.

I had to stop reading for a moment. I closed the journal and pressed my palms against my eyes, trying to block out the emotion welling up inside me. *No wonder he's the way he is.* No wonder he's so hard and closed off. He's had no role models, no one to show him what love or compassion looks like.

After a few minutes, I forced myself to continue. The following entries were about his teenage years. Dawson wrote about working odd jobs, anything he could get his hands on, just to make ends meet. I'd assumed he was always privileged, but he spent endless nights scrubbing floors, delivering newspapers, and even working at a garage just to help his mother keep the lights on. He was the one holding everything together.

Then, the part that made my stomach turn was his father. Dawson had written about how his father beat him and his mother, how he would come home drunk and angry, fists flying at anything and anyone in his path. His mother didn't fight back. She just took it, crumbling under his fists. Even as a child, Dawson tried to protect her, but he was small, and his father was relentless.

I wanted to go to his house and scream at them all. How could they do this to him? To a child? To their own flesh and blood?

But it didn't stop there. Dawson's journals chronicled the downward spiral of his father's health. The man had a heart attack, and his business, the very thing that Dawson now runs, was on the brink of collapse. Dawson's mother wanted to sell it off and get rid of it before it bankrupted them. But Dawson, still just a young man, had begged her not to. He took over the business, hoping to make it a success and hoping to save his father from more stress.

While his father was in the hospital and his mother was spiraling into her own depression, Dawson managed *everything*. He paid for her hospitalizations when she tried to kill herself, terrified of a life without her husband, and visited her every day while his brothers did *nothing*. They stood on the sidelines, watching Dawson struggle to keep the family afloat.

When his father recovered and his mother was released from the hospital, Dawson told them the good news: the business was turning around. Thanks to him, it was doing better than ever. But instead of pride or gratitude, his father saw it as a blow to his ego. He shunned Dawson even more, insulted that his son had succeeded where he had failed.

That was when Dawson decided to leave. He moved away, determined to make something of himself, not for his father's approval, but because he wanted to be better, to rise above the life they had given him. He restructured the family business, making it entirely his own and pouring everything he had into the hotels. After making his fortune, he even tried to help his parents, sending them money and buying them a new house—a gorgeous, sprawling estate. They refused to move in. They wanted nothing to do with his success.

The following entries in the journals covered his relationships. They all ended the same way. Every woman he let close eventually revealed they were more interested in his money than him. Each time he let himself believe that maybe this one would be different, he was wrong. They all wanted the lifestyle and the luxury, but none of them wanted Dawson Lancaster.

I swallowed hard, staring down at the pages in front of me. This was not the man I thought he was. Yes, he was cold, distant, and even arrogant, but it made sense now. He had built walls so high no one could see over them. He'd been hurt too many times by the people who were supposed to love him unconditionally.

Tears welled up in my eyes before I could stop them. I wiped my face angrily, frustrated with myself for feeling so much. This wasn't about me. This was his life and pain. But I couldn't help it. Everything I thought I knew about Dawson was crumbling away, revealing a man who had fought hard for everything he had and still felt like it wasn't enough.

I closed the journal gently, examining the leather cover. How was I supposed to look at him the same way now? How was I supposed to go back to writing this biography without pouring all of this emotion into it?

I felt a rush of anger toward his parents, brothers, and every single person who had ever hurt him. I wanted to march up to his father and scream at him for being too proud to see what an incredible son he had. I wanted to demand that his brothers acknowledge all Dawson had done for them.

But none of that would change what had happened. None of it would heal the wounds they had left behind.

I sat back, staring at the garden, my mind a whirlwind of thoughts. Dawson had said he didn't want to see me until I had finished reading, and now that I had, I wasn't sure what to do next.

One thing was clear, though: I didn't hate him anymore. I didn't even dislike him. If anything, my heart broke for him.

***

It took me all day to finish reading Dawson's journals. Every page was a revelation, peeling back layers of the man I thought I knew. My heart ached for him in ways I hadn't expected. When I finally closed the last journal, I knew I had to find him. I needed to see him.

I walked out to the pool, and there he was, as usual, floating in the water like he was trying to escape from the world. Without a word, I stripped down and slid into the pool, swimming toward him. When I reached him, I kissed him softly at first, then with more urgency and passion.

He pulled back, eyes dark with emotion. "I don't want your pity, Kansas."

I shook my head, my heart pounding. "It's not pity, Dawson. It's not."

Before he could say anything else, I kissed him again, pouring everything I felt into that moment. He didn't resist. Our bodies tangled together in the water, igniting the need between us.

Dawson crushed his lips to mine, then turned me around so he could slide his hands up to my breasts and finger the nipples until they hardened. I groaned against him as I turned my head to catch his lips again.

"I want you," I whispered breathlessly.

Dawson said nothing, but he didn't have to. I could feel him fill me deep inside, and as he thrust, I simply lost control. Heat flooded my center, and I crashed at the same time he did. We clung together, the water lapping around us while the world faded away.

Later, we went to his room and slept in each other's arms. It was the most peaceful sleep I had in weeks.

Chapter 16:

Dawson

The late afternoon sun reflected off the crystal-clear water, casting ripples of light across the poolside. Kansas sat beside me, scribbling notes into her journal as we reviewed the book's final chapters. For once, things felt peaceful. There were no biting remarks or lingering resentment. It was as if the weight of my past, which I'd finally shared with her, had softened something between us.

She glanced at me, her lips curving into a small, rare smile. "You know, Dawson, I never expected to like writing your story," she admitted, her voice soft.

I leaned back in my chair, smiling at the progress between us. "I never expected you'd give me the chance to tell it."

There was a charged silence between us, but it wasn't uncomfortable. It felt like everything had shifted—like we were finally on the same page.

"Let's take a break," I suggested, nodding toward the pool. Kansas hesitated, then stood, peeling off her sundress, revealing the bikini underneath. My breath hitched, but I kept calm, following her into the water.

The cool water rushed over us, a perfect contrast to the heat in the air. We swam closer, our bodies brushing against each other, until she stopped, her gray eyes meeting mine. One look was all it took.

Our lips met, slow at first, but the kiss deepened, the desire between us building. Before I knew it, I had her pressed against the edge of the pool, my hands tangling in her wet hair, and we were lost in the moment, lost in each other.

"I'm falling for you, Kansas," I whispered in her ear.

She shivered in delight and said, "I'm falling for you too. I want you."

"I need you," I confessed. "You're everything I think about." I leaned down to claim her lips, pulling her closer. Even though we were in the refreshing pool, I could feel the heat between us.

"Make love to me," Kansas murmured between kisses.

"I thought you'd never ask," I said with a grin as I pulled her up, and she wrapped her legs around my torso. I reached down and slipped my fingers inside, wanting to get her wet for me, as I kissed her passionately. Moments later, I was thrusting inside her as we found our perfect rhythm. I'd made love with several women, but being with Kansas was out of this world. I reached up and grasped her breasts just as I orgasmed. She threw her head back as she joined me, her eyes wild with desire.

For the first time in a long time, it felt like everything was exactly where it needed to be.

Just as I pulled Kansas closer to kiss her again, a sharp voice shattered the moment.

"Dawson!"

I froze, turning to see Lara standing at the edge of the pool, her face twisted in shock and fury. Kansas immediately pulled away, her jaw-dropping.

"You're *cheating* on me?!" Lara shrieked with anger. "How could you do this to me? I thought we were getting married and having babies!"

I blinked, still processing her words. "Lara, we're not—"

"Save it!" she screamed, pointing at Kansas. "Is this who you've been seeing behind my back?!"

Kansas stood silently, confusion and shock swarming her features.

I scrambled out of the pool, water dripping off me as I rushed toward Lara, who was now in full-blown hysterics. "Lara, stop!" I hissed, trying to quiet her down, but she was already spiraling.

Her eyes were wild, tears streaking down her face as she pointed a trembling finger at me. "How could you, Dawson?" she cried, her voice breaking. "How could you do this to me? After everything?"

"Lara, you need to calm down," I said, my voice low but firm, hoping to avoid causing a scene. Kansas stood frozen by the pool, watching the train wreck unfold.

Lara stepped closer, fists clenched, and before I could react, she started hitting me, her small hands pounding against my chest. "I love you! I *know* you still love me too! You don't get to just walk away like this!"

I caught her wrists gently, holding her still. "Lara, we were never—"

"Don't lie to me!" she screamed, wrenching her hands-free. "What about Tuscany? What about what we shared when you and *her* came out there?" She spat the word 'her,' glaring at Kansas with venom in her eyes.

Kansas stiffened at the mention, clearly taken aback. I felt a knot tighten in my gut as I realized how bad this looked.

"What we shared? Lara, that was—" I began, but she cut me off.

"You know exactly what I'm talking about! That afternoon we spent together." Lara's voice lowered, but the accusation dripped from every word. She shot Kansas a look of pure disgust. "After *that* afternoon, and now you're with *her*?"

Kansas' eyes flickered with hurt and confusion, her face pale. I knew I had to fix this, but the damage was already done.

I stepped closer to Lara, lowering my voice to keep things contained. "Lara, you know why we were together that day," I said sharply.

Her lips trembled, and she shook her head violently. "We were supposed to be together! I *know* you feel it too. You can't just throw me away."

I sighed, feeling the weight of her words and the wreckage of what had been a fleeting connection in Tuscany. Kansas looked like she was about to walk away, and I couldn't let that happen.

"Lara, let's meet for dinner. We can talk about this then," I told her, my voice demanding.

Lara let out a choked sob, stumbling back as the reality hit her. "You two-timing asshole!"

I turned to Kansas, guilt washing over me. She didn't speak, but the hurt in her eyes said it all.

"Lara, calm down," I said, trying to keep my voice steady, though the situation was spiraling fast. Her chest heaved, eyes wild with anger and heartbreak.

I turned to Kansas, who stood awkwardly by the pool, clearly uncomfortable. "Would you mind giving us some privacy?" I asked, hoping she'd understand.

"Of course," Kansas replied, her voice clipped but polite. She gathered up all our papers, her movements deliberate, and avoided looking at either of us.

She left without another word, leaving me standing there, trying to figure out how to untangle the mess Lara had just thrown us into.

I turned back to Lara, her sobs quieting as she sat down on one of the patio chairs, shaking. I sat beside her, trying to remain calm, though everything about this moment felt like walking on eggshells.

"I love you, Dawson," she whispered, her voice raw. "I'm sorry I cheated on you. I was confused, but I never stopped loving you."

I sighed, running a hand through my wet hair. "Lara, we've been over this. I'm not in love with you anymore."

Her eyes filled with panic, and she grabbed my hand, her grip tight. "No! Don't say that. You don't mean it. I'm sorry I told you I only wanted you for your money. I didn't mean it. I promise." Her voice broke, and for a moment, I almost believed her. She seemed so lost.

I kept my voice gentle, though my heart raced. "It really doesn't matter anymore. I overcame what you did to me, and I've moved on."

Tears spilled down her cheeks. "I thought I was getting over you," she sobbed. "I thought I could move on. But seeing you again just reminded me how much I still love you, Dawson. How much I need you."

I stayed silent momentarily, knowing this conversation would be difficult no matter what I said. "Lara," I started slowly, "what we had—it's over. It's been over for a long time."

Her shoulders shook as she wiped her face. "But Tuscany, we were there together. You went with me to see my dad, knowing he was dying. You stayed with me and comforted me. You were so attentive and sweet. I thought that meant you still cared about me and that we would find our way back to each other."

Tuscany. That afternoon had been heavy, standing by her side as her father lay in his bed, knowing it was the last time she would see him alive. I had gone because she needed a friend. But to Lara, it had meant something more.

"I was with you that day because you needed me as a friend. Nothing more. You're reading far too much into that."

She shook her head, gripping my hand tighter. "Please, Dawson. Please give me another chance. I'll be better. We can fix things."

I took a deep breath, pulling my hand away gently. "I'm with Kansas now. I care about her."

The words seemed to break her, and her sobs grew louder. "Kansas?" she spat. "You're *leaving* me for her?"

I stood, feeling the weight of her grief. "We were never back together. I'm sorry, Lara. I'm going to have to ask you to leave now."

After Lara left, I rushed to Kansas' room, eager to explain everything and to clear up the mess Lara had caused. My heart pounded as I reached the door, but I froze when I pushed it open.

The room was empty.

Her clothes, her bags—everything was gone.

I stood there, stunned, unable to move. She had left.

"Kansas?" I called out, hoping she was still nearby, but only silence greeted me.

She was gone, and my heart shattered into a million pieces.

Chapter 17:

Kansas

I stumbled into the house, dropping my suitcase with a loud thud. My sisters, Mindy and Alyssa, were in the kitchen, clearly startled by the noise. When they turned to look at me, their eyes widened in unison.

"Uh oh," Alyssa breathed, setting down the mug she'd been holding. "What happened?"

I swallowed, trying to find the words. I felt like I was about to shatter into a thousand pieces. "It's over. I'm done. I left Dawson."

Mindy raised an eyebrow, her eyes sharp behind her glasses. "Judging by the look on your face, I would have to say good riddance," she said a little too quickly, crossing her arms over her chest. "He was a pompous ass anyway."

Alyssa tilted her head and frowned, her soft eyes full of concern. "Kansas, maybe you should go back and talk to him. Sometimes things aren't what they seem." She stepped forward, placing a gentle hand on my shoulder. "You've worked so hard on that book. Are you sure this is really what you want?"

I shook my head, feeling a lump form in my throat. "I can't, Alyssa. He's everything I hate. He's rich, arrogant, and a womanizer! Whenever I think I can get past it, he does something else that reminds me we're from different worlds."

Mindy snorted, grabbing her tea from the counter. "Sounds like he did you a favor. You've been unhappy since you started working with him. You don't need that kind of negativity in your life." She took a sip, watching me closely, her tone matter-of-fact. "You're better off without him, Kansas. Let him marry one of those gold diggers his mom's always parading around."

I let out a dry laugh, even though it hurt. "Trust me, I'm not his type. But it wasn't just him, Mindy. It's me. I let all those walls come crashing down. I actually thought I was starting to understand him, that maybe he wasn't as bad as I thought." I sank into a chair at the kitchen table, burying my face in my hands as the tears finally spilled over. "I'm such an idiot."

Alyssa sat down beside me, wrapping an arm around my shoulders. "You're not an idiot. You're human. You have feelings. Maybe you just need time to process everything."

"Or maybe," Mindy interrupted, her tone crisp, "you should realize he's not worth your time. You've worked your ass off to get where you are, Kansas. You don't need some ultra-rich jerk making you feel less them." She gave a small huff.

I groaned, pulling my hands away from my face. "It's not that simple. He's complicated. He has these moments where I don't know. I see something real underneath all that arrogance, which messes with my head. Then, the next minute, he's back to being Dawson Lancaster, hotel king of the world and womanizer, who has everything handed to him on a silver platter."

Mindy rolled her eyes. "Rich men and their silver platters. They've got no idea what it's like to work for anything."

Alyssa sighed. "Mindy, you're not helping." She looked at me with those big, hopeful eyes. "Kansas, are you sure it's over? Maybe you two just need to talk things out. You've spent so much time together. He can't be all bad if you were considering dating him."

I shrugged, feeling overwhelmed. "He had a tough childhood, and it made me see a whole different side of him, and then he goes and cheats on me. I don't get it," I moaned.

"Oh, really?" Mindy asked. "What happened?"

I took a deep breath, feeling the weight of everything I'd read in Dawson's journals settle heavily on my chest. Mindy and Alyssa sat at the kitchen table, waiting for me to explain. They watched me closely, waiting for me to explain the whirlwind of emotions swirling inside me.

"You know, Dawson isn't who I thought he was," I began. "I've spent all this time thinking he was just some arrogant, privileged billionaire, but after reading his journals, I now know he's been through hell."

Alyssa's brows furrowed, concern washing over her face. "What do you mean?"

I swallowed hard. "His childhood was awful. He grew up in this rundown neighborhood, with cracked sidewalks and houses practically falling apart. His mom wasn't cold and distant like when I met her. She was broken—panic attacks, depression, violent outbursts. She was in and out of mental institutions for most of his life."

Mindy crossed her arms, her skepticism fading. "Seriously?"

"He wrote about how he'd sit in their tiny living room, waiting for her to come back from the hospital, hoping this time would be different. But it never was. He had to hold her, Alyssa, when she was at her worst—crying in his arms until she fell asleep. And he was just a kid, feeling like he had to take care of her."

Alyssa's eyes filled with tears. "That's heartbreaking."

"It gets worse," I said, my voice thick. "His dad was violent and abusive. He would come home drunk and take his anger out on Dawson and his mom. His brothers weren't any better. They bullied him and ganged up on him whenever they could. He wrote about hiding in his room at night, locking himself in, just trying to stay invisible."

Mindy's eyes darkened, and she shook her head. "No wonder he's so closed off."

"Exactly," I whispered. "He's never known love, not real love. His teenage years were spent working odd jobs—scrubbing floors, delivering newspapers—just to keep the lights on. He wasn't born into privilege like I thought. He clawed his way out of that life. His father never even thanked him when he turned their failing business into the massive hotel empire it is now. Instead, he resented him for succeeding where he had failed."

Alyssa wiped a tear from her cheek. "I had no idea."

"Neither did I," I said softly. "And now, I don't know how to look at him the same way. It made me think differently about him and now." I closed my eyes to push back the tears. "Now, I don't know what to think with this whole Lara thing." I took a deep breath, wiping my eyes. "Look, if Dawson shows up here, don't let him in. I don't want to see him. Not yet. I need space to figure this out. Promise me you won't answer the door, or if you do, tell him I'm not here." I hated asking my sisters to lie for me, but I just didn't have the mind space to deal with him.

Both of them nodded, but while Mindy's agreement was firm, Alyssa's was more hesitant.

"We'll give you space, Kansas," Alyssa said softly. "But don't close the door completely, okay? You need to hear him out. He deserves that, at least. Sometimes people surprise you."

"Yeah," I mumbled, exhausted. "I've had enough surprises to last me a lifetime."

***

A few hours later, I sat in my car outside Shellene's place. I grabbed my phone and texted her that I was there.

The door opened before I even knocked. Shellene stood there, her eyes soft and welcoming, like always. "Kansas, come in. I made us some tea."

I stepped inside, the familiar warmth of her cozy little first-floor apartment easing some of my tension. The scent of jasmine filled the air, and I instantly felt calmer.

We settled onto her couch, and she handed me a mug of tea. "So," she said, smiling gently, "what's happening? You sounded like you needed to talk."

I took a deep breath, staring down at the steam rising from my cup. "I left him."

Shellene raised her eyebrows, but she didn't look surprised. "Dawson?"

I nodded. "Yeah. I packed up and walked out. I thought I was doing the right thing, you know? I couldn't stand being around him, knowing he was with his ex, Lara."

"He was with his ex?" she prompted, her voice soft.

I swallowed hard, feeling the words catch in my throat. "Yes, but I have a problem. I think I'm falling in love with him."

Shellene's expression softened even more, and she leaned back on the couch, crossing her legs. "Kansas, what's in your heart matters more than anything. If you're falling in love with him, then it's real. What makes you so sure, though?"

I hesitated, my mind spinning with everything I'd read in his journals and learned about him. "I saw a side of him no one else sees. He's been through so much, Shellene. His childhood and struggles growing up. It explains why he's the way he is. And now, I don't know how to stop feeling this way, even though I know it's a bad idea."

Shellene took a sip of her tea, then set it down carefully. "Love is never a bad idea. But what about your book? You won't get that big payout if you don't finish it."

I sighed, feeling the weight of it all pressing down on me. "I know. I think I've got enough to finish it now, so I don't need to be with him anymore. It would've been better if I stayed longer, but I can make it work."

"Then do it," she said, her voice firm but encouraging. "Finish the book. I'm sure if you need to talk to him, you can do it through emails."

I smiled, feeling a spark of determination light inside me. "You're right. I'll finish the book and just work on forgetting him."

"If it's meant to be, it will," Shellene reminded me. "You can't escape your fate."

I rolled my eyes. "Fate? I highly doubt it's that. I will have a bubble bath when I get home to soothe my nerves."

"Let's watch a movie first—a thriller to take our mind off men," she suggested.

"Sounds like the perfect idea."

I came home around midnight and sank into the hot, bubbly water, letting the warmth envelop me. My phone lay discarded on the counter, completely turned off. For the first time in what felt like forever, I was unreachable, which felt liberating. A few tears slipped down my cheeks as I rested my head on the edge of the tub, allowing the sadness to flow.

After what seemed like hours, I wrapped myself in a towel and retreated to my room. I turned on an old rerun of *Friends*, hoping it would lift my spirits. I looked at my phone, tempted to turn it off, but decided better of it. I needed this—peace. Finally, I curled up in bed and drifted off to the sounds of laughter from the TV.

Chapter 18:

Dawson

I pulled up to Kansas' house, nerves buzzing through my veins. Her sisters, Mindy and Alyssa, opened the door as if they'd been expecting me.

"Hello. My name is Dawson Lancaster. Is Kansas here?" I asked, trying to keep my voice steady.

Mindy shook her head, but I could see the lie flicker in her eyes. Alyssa shifted uncomfortably beside her, biting her lip.

"She's not home, Dawson," Alyssa said, her voice too sweet, too high. "Sorry."

I exhaled slowly, glancing between them. "Look, I know she's upset, and I get it. But you both need to know the truth. That afternoon with Lara was not what it seemed like." Their expressions softened slightly. "Lara's father passed away. He was like family to me, and I was just being a good friend to her, but she thought it was more. I assure you, it wasn't."

Mindy crossed her arms, skeptical but listening. "And Lara? What about her?"

"She's manipulative, trying to use her grief to drive a wedge between me and Kansas," I said, frustration building. "But I swear, I never cheated. I'm in love with Kansas and have just realized I can't live without her." I felt my throat tighten. "I need your help. Please. Can you please get her to a restaurant tonight for 6 p.m.?"

They exchanged glances before Mindy nodded, her analytical gaze softening. "We'll get her there."

Later that afternoon, I was a wreck, pacing around the restaurant as I prepped every detail. Mindy and Alyssa came and helped decorate the room with Kansas' favorite flowers—dahlias. The pinks and reds filled the room with warmth and hope, and all I could do was pray that tonight, Kansas would understand. That tonight, she'd forgive me.

"Thank you, ladies. I really appreciate your help," I told them as they hugged me goodbye.

"Good luck, Dawson. You just might need it," Minda said with a shake of her head.

Alyssa was more enthusiastic. "She's going to melt like putty in your hands."

***

By the time 6:30 p.m. rolled around, I was practically pacing holes in the floor. Every minute that passed felt like an eternity. The chef gave me a sympathetic look as I asked him to keep everything warm again. The candlelit table was set perfectly with her favorite flowers. Everything was exactly as I'd planned, except for one thing: Kansas wasn't there.

At 6:45, I checked my phone again, though I hadn't expected a text. Kansas wasn't the type to send a warning if she wasn't coming. At 6:50, I let out a long breath and sat down. Maybe I'd pushed too hard. Maybe she was done with me for good.

I was about to tell the chef to wrap everything up when the door opened, and there she was. Kansas. She looked radiant in a simple, soft pink summer dress, her hair falling in soft waves around her shoulders. My heart stopped for a beat—how could she make me feel like this?

I stood, moving toward her without thinking, my arms instinctively reaching out. "Kansas—"

But she pulled away, her expression cool, distant. "Dawson."

The space between us felt like a canyon, and I cursed myself for letting it get to this point. "I'm sorry," I began, my voice low. "I never meant to hurt you. Lara was trying to drive us apart. Her father passed away, and I was just trying to be a friend. But she manipulated everything into something it wasn't."

Kansas stayed quiet, her eyes searching mine, waiting for more.

"I would never cheat on you. Never. I care about you too much, Kansas. You're the one I—" I stopped, realizing the words that almost slipped out. "I don't want to lose you."

She just looked at me for a long moment, her face unreadable. Then, slowly, the tension in her shoulders eased. "I didn't want to believe it, but seeing you with her hurt. Why didn't you just tell me that day in Tuscany? Then, none of this would have happened."

I swallowed hard, nodding. "I should've told you sooner. I was just trying to forget about it, figuring my relationship with Lara was over, and it didn't matter."

Kansas took a deep breath and stepped closer, her walls falling even just a little. "I misjudged you. I didn't give you a chance to explain, and I'm sorry for that."

Relief flooded through me as I gestured to the table. "Stay for dinner? Please?"

She hesitated but nodded, taking a seat. As we ate, the conversation flowed easily, and by the end of the meal, it felt like we had turned a corner. She smiled softly, and I knew, maybe—just maybe—I hadn't lost her after all.

Dinner with Kansas was perfect. We talked about everything—her writing, my hotels, even random things like our favorite movies. At one point, we ended up laughing so hard that I thought I might choke on my drink. The tension from earlier had melted away, replaced by something warmer and genuine.

As we finished dessert, I couldn't take it any longer. I stood and walked around the table, pulling her up gently into my arms. Her body fit perfectly against mine, and before I could second-guess myself, I kissed her deeply and passionately. I poured every emotion I had for her into that kiss.

When I finally pulled back, breathless, I said, "Kansas, I'm in love with you. I've loved you for longer than I realized, and I can't imagine my life without you."

Her eyes softened as she placed a hand on my cheek. "Dawson, I love you too. I was so wrong to judge you without really knowing you. You're everything I didn't know I needed."

We hugged tightly, and everything felt lighter. I leaned in close, whispering, "We should head back to my place to continue the celebrating."

Kansas raised an eyebrow, smirking. "Any other women going to crash our lovemaking sessions?"

I chuckled, holding her closer. "Only, um, NONE!"

She laughed, and together, we headed out, ready to start the next chapter of our story.

***

As we drove to my place, Kansas brought up the book. "We still have a lot to do. It's not finished."

I smiled, glancing at her. "We'll finish it and polish it together. No rush."

She nodded, her fingers tracing the edge of the seat. "You really think people will care about your story?"

I chuckled. "Care? Kansas, we already have over 150,000 pre-orders."

Her eyes widened. "You're serious?"

"Dead serious. People want to know the real story behind Lancaster Luxury Estates." I reached over, squeezing her hand. "And you're the only one who can tell it right. I'll get you your $300,000 bank draft on Monday so you can start making arrangements."

"Arrangements?"

"Selling your house," I reminded her. "I'd love to help you pick out your new place. I mean, I'm going to have to love it since I hope to spend a lot of time there with you."

She blushed, and I couldn't wait to get her to my bedroom.

We barely got in the front door before she was clawing at me to take my clothes off.

"So feisty! I think I'm going to like this side of you," I murmured as I kissed behind her ear and down her neck to her collarbone.

Kansas backed me up to the oversized sofa, and we fell onto it, kissing each other with pent-up sexual frustration.

"I have servants, in case you've forgotten," I reminded her.

She looked at me with wide eyes, then got off the sofa and extended her hand. "Shall we take this upstairs then?"

I stood and then picked her up to carry her. She shrieked and yelled, "Dawson! Put me down!"

"Not a chance. You were walking far too slow."

Once we got to my room, I closed and locked the door and lowered her onto the bed. "I want you, Kansas Stonehouse. More than I've ever wanted anyone in my life."

"Then take me," she whispered breathlessly.

I lay on top of her and kissed her sensually. "It seems we're not quite naked." I rose up on my knees and removed her bra and panties, then took my briefs off and mounted her. She looked up at me and giggled as she reached up to pull me down.

Within seconds, I was deep inside her, and we were moving together, each of us needing the other more than we could ever say. I laced my fingers with her and drew them above her head as I bent my head to take a fleshy mound in my mouth. I rolled her nipple between my teeth and pushed in further. When I withdrew, she gasped and called out my name, which resulted in me thrusting in even deeper.

"Dawson, please! I can't stand it any longer," she cried as we rode the wave of passion up and down until we both released together. I could feel her tighten against me as she threw her head back and closed her eyes. I was still, and I could feel myself throb as I came down from the moment of bliss with her.

We clung to each other after, our breaths rising and falling as our hearts slowed back into their natural rhythms.

I feathered kisses on her cheek and over her perfect nose. "Would you want to get married and have children someday?"

She gave me a bewildered look and smiled. "Right now?"

I laughed and kissed her lips softly. "No, silly. In the future. Is that a life goal of yours?"

"Yes, what about you?"

"Only if it's you I get to marry and have little Kansas' running all over the house."

"What about little Dawson's?"

I raised an eyebrow. "That's a lot of children. I guess you'll have to move into the mansion with me so we can get started."

Her eyes grew huge. "You want me to move in here?"

I nodded. "It seems the right thing to do."

She smiled, and her eyes twinkled. "I don't know. This place is pretty small, and you know how I like my space." I knew she was just teasing.

I rolled my eyes. "We'll build another wing or two. Just how many kids are we having?"

"About six or more," she teased.

"Wow. We're going to be busy!"

"I love you, Dawson Lancaster."

"I love you too, Mrs. Kansas Lancaster."

"Someday in our future, I will respond to that name," she said with a grin.

We laughed and embraced each other, never wanting to let go.

www.ingramcontent.com/pod-product-compliance
Lightning Source LLC
Chambersburg PA
CBHW021634120626
46545CB00002B/543